*"Travel and passion go t
bringing passion to life i
days to our shared indust.*
as pent-up demand starts to ignite people's inherent passion to explore the world. Not everyone will benefit equally from this coming resurgence, those who focus on continuous education, knowledge and learning will lead the charge. **Flying Colours: The Travel Advisor's Guide to Breakthrough**, is a wonderful building block in ensuring you are at the forefront of travel's great comeback."*

~ Andy Stuart, Past President, Norwegian Cruise Line

*"Any travel advisor looking to take their business to the next level should read this book. I've always been inspired by Geraldine's passion for travel advisors and their success is at the forefront of everything she does. She is a proven leader having worked in the travel industry in many capacities and has a unique perspective of what it takes to be successful and how to get there. What stands out is that **Flying Colours** is written exclusively for Travel Advisors — a rare read."*

~ Steve Smotrys, Vice President, Seabourn

"No matter how much tenure we have in any business, no matter our reputation, no matter our skill set, we are still capable of opening our hearts to learning more – especially from our colleagues. We call it best practices. Geraldine knows of what she speaks and teaches on this incredible journey.

Geraldine has "nailed" the essence of why we continue to love our industry, at the same time we need to strengthen our skills by having a full plan in place.

*I love this book. **Flying Colours** will teach you what you need to know about your personal breakthrough so you come out stronger, bolder and more confident than ever."*

~ Cathy Denroche, Regional Sales Director, Oceania Cruises

Insightful, thoughtful and meaningful...just like Geraldine Ree!

Flying Colours *is a terrific book for all travel advisors, at all levels! Each chapter will give you a new idea to implement and you'll have fun reading it over and over! Geraldine captivates the auspicious and complicated role of the travel advisor and her keen understanding of the travel industry brings focus to the practicality of her ideas. Having had the wonderful experience of working with Geraldine, it gives me great pleasure to recommend* Flying Colours!

~ Anne Marie Moebes, Publisher, Travel Market Report

"As an entrepreneur, I feel privileged to have been able to pursue my passion and be surrounded by exceptionally talented and genuine people in the travel industry who have found their purpose in life.

One such person that I have had the great pleasure of working with over many years is Geraldine Ree. She is a true champion of lifelong learning. I can't think of a more qualified and compassionate person to provide the practical advice, creative thinking and positive support needed to help others in the travel industry move out of their comfort zone and pursue the goals that will take their business to a new level.

While these are challenging times, I believe that from great challenges come great opportunities! I encourage you to read ***Flying Colours****. This book provides the guidance, tools and reassurance needed to create a more rewarding and satisfying travel career and personal life balance. As Geraldine so aptly quotes Dolly Parton: Pour yourself a cup of ambition!"*

~ Kristin Karst, Co-owner, AMA Waterways

*"****Flying Colours*** *is a must for Travel Advisors. This book will be your go-to guide for successfully breaking through the next season of your business.*

For years Geraldine has focused on enabling Travel Advisors to not just succeed but to thrive. She is laser focused on empowering individuals to see their strengths and identify the shift that you need to make to level up your business.

Travel advisors have navigated through the toughest time in the industry. You now have the opportunity and access to Geraldine's systematic approach to ensure your actions are purposeful and focused on future growth.

Geraldine's passion and dedication to the travel industry shines through with this must-read book."

~ Caroline Hay, National Director, Sales & Marketing, TPI

Geraldine has done it, it's a must read for travel agents ready to grow their travel business in a post COVID world. The opportunity has never been greater, full of practical tips to take advantage of the coming travel rebound!

I have been lucky enough to be able to receive guidance from Geraldine on the growth of my multi center agency. I have always been impressed with her industry knowledge combined with a passion for sales.

~ Shawn Friesen, Expedia Cruises, Franchise Partner

Knowing Geraldine for over 20 years, I can say without hesitation what a champion she is for the travel advisor community. Her passion and enthusiasm not only inspire those she knows — they have a true impact on our industry. One of the many things I love about Geraldine is her appreciation for training and education to enhance the value travel advisors bring to their clients.

This book is a testament to that appreciation and will serve as a great resource.

~ Vicki Freed, SVP Sales and Trade Support & Service, Royal Caribbean International

Flying Colours

The Travel Advisor's Guide to Breakthrough

Geraldine Ree

First published in 2021 by Hambone Publishing
Melbourne, Australia

Book design and layout: Sadie Butterworth-Jones
Cover design: Valentina Carta

For information about this title, please contact:
Geraldine Ree
www.geraldineree.com

Paperback ISBN 978-1-7775848-2-5
eBook ISBN 978-1-7775848-3-2

Dedication

This book is dedicated to my mother, Beatrice Durrant. She was my role model for perseverance, resilience, and a sense of humor, each of which she had beyond measure.

My mother encouraged me with every breath she took.

She was the namesake of Durrant House, a women's shelter, named in her honor after she and my father, Bob Durrant gave 17 years of selfless service.

My parents laid out wisdom for me like breadcrumbs on the path to significance.

This quote hung on a wall in our home in West Vancouver, BC in 1975:

Persistence

Nothing in this world can take the place of persistence. Talent will not; nothing is more common than unsuccessful men with talent. Genius will not; unrewarded genius is almost a proverb. Education will not; the world is full of educated derelicts. Persistence and determination alone are omnipotent.

~ ***Calvin Coolidge***

Never underestimate the power of a well-placed source of inspiration.

I've never forgotten it.

Acknowledgements

To my husband-love, Cam. I owe my deepest gratitude for believing in me, suggesting I write the book, and helping me across the finish line. This book, as with my life, would not have been possible or any fun without you!

To my children and grandchildren. Gillian & Mark, Travis, Jamieson, Henry and James, I love you and I'm deeply inspired by each one of you.

To my family. More! More! More!

Last but not least, I wish to acknowledge the long list of remarkable agency owners and advisors whom I've had the privilege of working with over the last thirty years.

Your passion, commitment and dedication to excellence inspired me to write this book.

Your astonishing perseverance and resilience to get through even the darkest of times, encouraged me to get it published.

Contents

Introduction 1

Chapter 1: Mindset Shift 17

Chapter 2: The Customer Shift — Part One 43

Chapter 3: The Customer Shift — Part Two 61

Chapter 4: The Sales Shift 97

Chapter 5: The Performance Shift — Part One 131

Chapter 6: The Performance Shift — Part Two 141

Conclusion 189

About the Author 193

Introduction

Travel opens our eyes and expands our hearts as we experience the people, culture, and history of the world. Travel is a magnificent gift to celebrate the milestones in our lives. We look forward to it with childlike anticipation. The more we travel, the more we appreciate the things we take for granted. We simply cannot wait to travel again.

The travel industry is home. It's been my home for over thirty years. It's home to one in ten people in the global work force. Airlines, hotels, cruise lines, tour operators, transportation, and travel distribution make up the complex infrastructure of our industry. Travel advisors are the vital link that enable the flow of customers throughout the ecosystem.

I firmly believe that travel customers are best served in the hands of a travel professional. Travel advisors are the backbone of this industry and the future of travel depends on their success.

If you're reading this book, your passion for working in the travel industry runs deep within you. For you, working in the travel industry is so much more than a job, a business, or a career. It's a way of life.

I share that passion with you! What stands out for me about the travel industry is the people who work in it. Travel people are special. They share a passion for making dreams come true for people through travel. They genuinely love what they do. When times are good, they cheer each other on. When times are tough, they pull together and support one another.

The pandemic of 2020 will mark the most significant setback in the history of our industry. The virus brought the travel industry to a complete halt, resulting in catastrophe and chaos. Some of us in travel have lost loved ones. We've seen heartbreaking closures, furloughs and layoffs. Worse yet, loss and isolation continue and uncertainty rages on.

I am not a medical expert or an economist, but one thing I know for certain is that the world *will* travel again. In fact, I predict travel will have the greatest comeback of all time. It will be unlike anything we've seen before. It will be bigger in every sense of the word. It will be more precious to us, and more complex.

On the client side, the pre-pandemic desire for meaningful experiences over material things, will now be amplified. There will be an overwhelming need for handholding and detailed information regarding health and safety protocols during every segment of the travel experience. Travellers will require the kind of information that goes well beyond what you can find.

For travel advisors, you will need to put the safety and wellness of your clients at the forefront of every transaction. You will depend on reliable supplier partners and relationships more than ever before. The world will become smaller and — if you navigate your future accordingly — the new era of travel will be much more profitable for you.

This is your chance to make changes to *the way* you do travel business so you can make your mark on the travel industry rather than feeling like the industry is making its mark on you.

Looking back, you may have had this nagging thought: *this is too much work for the money*. I'm working harder than I ever have, but I'm still not getting the results I'm looking for. I don't mind working hard, but it's frustrating to put in all this time and not be where I was hoping or needing to be financially.

You are not alone. I've met thousands of incredible travel advisors who struggle with the same thought. I'm doing OK, but I could be earning more. Often a lower pay grade is being justified by the benefit of doing work you love, in the most exciting industry in the world. However, when the work becomes overwhelming, or an unreasonable client drains the last ounce of enthusiasm out of you, you start questioning whether it's all worth it.

Now, add in the new precautions and planning that will go into creating a vacation from start to finish. Each transaction will require more time and attention. The possibility of cancellations based on consumer confidence and uncertainty is going to be a constant. Soon, you will realize that adjustments need to be made to your approach, or you simply won't survive.

You may think it's not just about the money. And it's not, that's for certain. However, the difference between those who are wildly successful financially, and those who are doing OK or even those who are struggling, is not as big as you may think.

Earning more is also completely within your grasp. Looking ahead, it is possible to do more for the right group of clients, and to double or even triple your income. When you jump up a level in your business as a result of making a few small but significant shifts, the business is suddenly both fun *and* profitable.

The crossroad you're at now is a new one: *How can I transform my travel business to come out stronger and more successful than ever in this new era of travel?*

This book is your step-by-step guide to the other side of breakthrough in your travel business. This book will lead you through a simple process of finding, servicing, and retaining a steady stream of ideal customers. You'll know what is unique about you, who your people are, and how to reach them. You'll understand how to systematize the process to make it easy and elegant.

You will no longer feel like this business is way too much work for the money. Instead, your business will feel easy and flowing like it was always meant to be. It will feel like you were born for this. When you're doing your best work, the money *always* follows.

This book is a guide to your very personal and life-changing journey to breakthrough that starts from the moment you read the first chapter. It includes self-discovery, specialization, sales, and a system for optimizing your results. It's a path to doing more of the right things and letting go of the rest.

It's based on 30 years of experience, combined with a 360-degree view of the travel industry. It takes into consideration research, testimonials, and success stories from an entire ecosystem of stakeholders including frontline agents, suppliers, agency owners, hosts, and consortia leaders.

This book was also deeply inspired by observing highly skilled advisors firsthand, in the moment of truth when the stakes are high, delivering an exceptional customer experience. I've watched superstar advisors not just rise to the pinnacle of success financially, but continue to pay it forward and share their best practices with others.

I'm so excited you're here! I've been waiting a long time for you to arrive in this place. It means you're ready for a breakthrough. I'm ready to take you there.

My deepest wish is that this book will help you skill up and rise up beyond your wildest dreams and when you do, you'll share your experience with others.

Together, we can transform the industry and create a new, bolder approach to your travel business. You can be the change the industry is waiting for.

Let's do this, together!

If you're like most travel advisors, prior to the pandemic, you were struggling in one of the following four ways:

①   **You can't get on top of your business.**
There are not enough hours in the day to focus. You are reacting all the time. You can't get out from under the weight of getting everything done to create the kind of business you know you're capable of.

②   **You lack consistent, high-quality leads.**
You want more and better clients. You want highly appreciative clients. Instead, at times you find yourself wanting to scream in frustration at what clients expect you do to for them, or when a client leaves you for a lower price. It can be a feast of leads

one week and a famine the next.

3   **You lack enough experience to sell what you love.**
You haven't traveled enough, especially in the style
of travel your ideal clients are interested in. You
want to branch out and specialize, or up-sell to
luxury, but you can't get access to the right FAMs,
and don't have time or money to experience the right
travel products.

4   **You lack business expertise.**
The methods of attracting new and better clients
is beyond your skill set. You've tried a few things
on social media, created a newsletter or hosted an
event that took a lot of work, but they didn't produce
the results.

I firmly believe that you know what to do. You probably
even know how to do it, but despite your best-laid plans,
it has been almost impossible to rework and shift your
travel business.

The Four Forces Framework

If you're ready to transform your travel business into one
that is bigger, better and requires less work than you're
used to, this book has the answers you're looking for.
The **Four Forces Framework** is a systematic approach
to achieving remarkable results by turning chaos into
consistency. It will help you identify, focus, and deliver on
what matters, and confidently let go of the rest.

The pillars of the system are Mindset, Customer, Sales, and Performance. Let's review each one.

Mindset Shift

It starts with knowing yourself. It's a combination of your passion for the industry, your unique skills, and your deep knowledge of what customers want and need that sets you apart.

Customer Shift

A customer shift is moving from being all things to all people, to being everything to one important customer at a time. Customers need your undivided attention and sage wisdom every step of the way. As well, every vacationer is not your customer. Saying "no" to some customers will allow you room for a bigger "yes". As in yes, let's really do this right! More vacation energy, passion, and commitment *one customer at a time* is at the heart of your customer shift.

Sales Shift

Leading the customer journey from beginning to end through a series of deep and meaningful questions will help you customize their vacation solution. Selling *well* is the greatest customer service you can deliver.

Performance Shift

Setting goals and simplifying your process through mastery, delegation, and elimination leads to a dramatic change in your productivity. Skills and habits are a central theme to becoming a goal getter, not just a goal setter.

How to Read this Book and Soar with Flying Colours

The book identifies four shifts in order to achieve your travel business breakthrough. My belief is that it's never one thing but a series of small things done consistently well that will take you to your next level in your business.

While each shift is necessary, they are not required to be done in any order. While I recommend you read the book from start to finish, each shift can be worked at on its own. Don't wait to the end before you try things out in your own business. The sooner you start, the sooner you'll soar.

The Mindset Shift sets the context for what the book is about. How to cast an inspiring vision for yourself and your travel business, find your purpose, and identify who you serve.

The Customer Shift is two chapters — the first is about

identifying your ideal customer and the second is the who, what, where and why on communicating with them.

Next, if you're looking for sales tips, you can refer to the Sales Shift chapter multiple times as a reminder that there is always something about your sales game that you can learn more about and improve on.

Finally, you may want to dive right into the Performance Shift — if you're looking on how to set goals and make them stick.

I believe in you. I know you can do this. You've always known that you have this unique approach to selling travel. Now is the time to prepare for the future of travel by combining what you love with who you serve and how you serve them.

Becoming the "My" in My Travel Advisor

The ultimate goal as a travel advisor is to become the "My" in My Travel Advisor for a highly engaged group of ideal customers, one customer at a time.

Consider the services you have in your life that you refer to as "my" anything. "My Builder," if you're doing a home renovation. "My Coach," if you're working on self-improvement. "My Dry Cleaner", who can be in your life for years. Attaching the word "my" is the highest form of praise and loyalty. Your goal is to earn the distinction of My Travel Advisor for a community of raving fans.

Did you know that becoming "My Travel Advisor" for 250 loyal clients means you are running a multimillion-dollar travel business, doing work you love, with people you love.

Perhaps you dream of selling African safaris, Antarctic expeditions or filling small group charters to the South Pacific. Maybe your dream is to specialize in luxury travel and river cruises or sell tours to places you can only dream of, in a level of service you one day aspire to experience for yourself. Whatever it is, It's *all* there for you!

To become the "my" in "my travel advisor" is as simple and as difficult as narrowing your focus to identifying and attracting your ideal customer. One important customer, who brings out the very best in you.

You find yourself thinking about them all the time. If you attend a supplier seminar, and the product lights you up, you think of them. If you find a cool new travel experience online, you pop a video directly into their inbox. They are the first person you think of when needing a referral or a testimonial.

And from the client side, consider what they would need to think, feel, and believe about you before giving you this ultimate praise. Examine the following three factors:

First, they need to experience you, at your very best, every step of the way. From the instant they connect with you, throughout their travel experience, to when they return home, they need an imaginary checkbox that says, "My advisor did this for me".

An agent once shared with me a priceless thank you card. The cruise line was doing some in-transit repairs on the ship that her clients were traveling on. While her clients were in port, a painting crew went into her stateroom and changed the wall colour from a dark beige to a fresh white. The client wrote, "Thank you SO much for taking such good care of us! We couldn't believe it when you had our stateroom painted for us. We absolutely loved it!"

While this in fact was not initiated by the travel advisor but rather part of the regular ship maintenance, when you give a client the royal treatment, they will begin to think that you orchestrated every single element of their trip.

The second point that clients consider before giving you the title of 'my travel advisor' is, how you treated everyone. It's a big commitment for a client to refer a travel advisor to a close family member or friend. The moment you are given a referral you are going through an unspoken test with your client. Treat it with the kind of deference that is commensurate with the opportunity. If you pass with flying colours, future referrals will flow like a river, unlikely to be questioned again. Fail it, and it may cost you more than you will ever know.

Lastly, your most important customers need to know that

they have a special status with you. Like moving a romance from dating to a steady relationship, there needs to be a declarative moment when you say to your client, *"You are an important part of my inner circle"*.

Becoming "my travel advisor" to a deep pool of loyal customers is the gateway to your transformation. As we go through this book, the goal is to help you achieve this status with a steady stream of magnificent clients, booking a lifetime of travel.

Here we go!

Chapter Summary
Introduction

1. The Four Forces Framework is a systematic approach to achieving remarkable results by turning chaos into consistency.

2. The pillars of the system are Mindset, Customer, Sales, and Performance.

3. A Mindset Shift starts with knowing yourself. It is a combination of your vision, your purpose and who you choose to serve.

4. A customer shift is moving from being all things to all people, to being everything to one very important customer at a time.

5. A sales shift is leading the customer journey from beginning to end with deep meaningful questions.

6. The Performance Shift is when you make consistent steps towards continual improvement – every day, every week, and every month.

7. **My Travel Advisor**
   The goal as a travel advisor is to become the "My" in My Travel Advisor for a highly engaged group of ideal customers, one customer at a time.

8   A thriving travel business has you with between 250 and 500 loyal clients, earning more than six figures, and having time to enjoy the very thing you love – travel!

9   The three things that clients consider before giving you the "My Travel Advisor" title are:

- They experience the very best of you!
- How you treat the friends and family that they referred to you
- To feel appreciated by you.

Chapter 1
Mindset Shift

Think back to when you decided to become a travel advisor. It was significant because you made a decision to go in a new direction. Nobody made it for you. The opportunity may have presented itself but ultimately, it was your choice to take it. When you look back, chances are it was a series of choices, based on what you felt was important to you at the time, that created a single moment in time when you said, *"Yes, becoming a travel advisor is for me!"*.

A Mindset Shift is a choice. It's a moment in time where you decide, *"Let's do this!" "Let's go after this crazy goal. Let's sell millions of dollars of travel"* or, *"I'm going to be the most successful luxury advisor in my community!"*.

Sadly, we know that as quickly as those ideas spark inside us, they all too frequently fade away. You've been here before, on the verge of a breakthrough. However, unless you support that goal with concrete steps, decision becomes indecision, and you can wallow for a long time.

A Mindset Shift has everything you need to see this big idea through. It mobilizes thoughts into beliefs, beliefs into actions, and actions into results.

Mindset Shift is made up of three important elements:

①   First, you need a concrete vision of your future self that has already found the success you seek.

②   Next, you must be clear on your purpose, and act upon it, as if your business depends on it.

③   Finally, you must take a stand for who you will serve and how you will serve them.

A Mindset Shift is at the intersection of vision, purpose, and service. Let's explore each of these in more detail.

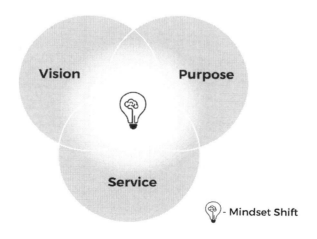

- Mindset Shift

 **Vision**

When you decided to become a travel advisor, you did not decide to become an *average* advisor. You likely did not picture yourself as an overwhelmed, tired, or anxious advisor. You pictured yourself as a fabulous, successful advisor! Perhaps you needed training, product knowledge, and experience, but that didn't hold you back from seeing yourself setting the world on fire because you were doing what you were passionate about!

Your breakthrough begins at that euphoric moment when you decide to go after the business you've always dreamed about and you create a clear vision of yourself achieving it.

The Mindset Shift includes a full-blown version of yourself, living out your vision like a motion picture of your dreams. The good news is that you get to be the director of this amazing movie: ***'My Brilliant Travel Business'.*** Not only do you get the starring role, you get to assign all of the cast members, choose the locations, and win the awards when it finally plays out in the world!

Twenty years ago, this happened to me. I landed my dream job. I was hired into a new leadership role that I had never done before. It was at least three levels above my past experience, and the first time I had ever led a team. To add to the pressure I put on myself, it was a newly created role, and I was the first woman to ever hold this position.

I was outwardly excited, but inwardly *terrified*. I had no clue how to do even half of what was in the job description. In other words, my vision of myself in this role, nervous, shaking and filled with uncertainty, was very different from what I wanted it to be — confident, relaxed and ready to deliver.

I knew that the only way forward was to start figuring things out. I found this quote and put it on a sticky note on my computer as a daily reminder of how to shift my mindset:

"The best way to predict your future is to create it."
*~ **Abraham Lincoln***

What stood out for me every time I read this quote, was that creating the future I wanted was completely within my control. When you start something new, there is SO much outside of your control. I couldn't change the fact that I lacked experience, or that I didn't have certain skills. What I could control, was taking the necessary steps to change that.

For as long as I could remember I had always wanted to be a leader. I began to create my vision of what this leader would look like with as much detail as possible. I learned from other great leaders, I studied leadership books, joined a leadership forum group, and learned the vital skills of empathy and listening. I worked hard day and night to put these lessons into practice.

My vision of what defines a great leader has transformed over the years, and become even more inspiring to me! While I'm still learning, I've grown from uncertain to certain, from disbelief to belief and eventually, to confident, relaxed, and ready to deliver.

Here are some suggestions to get you started on your vision of becoming the very best version of yourself:

- Describe your vision of a superstar travel advisor.

- How much will you sell?

- What destinations and experiences will be your specialties?

- What kind of clients will you serve?

- What do you hope clients will say about you?

- Who can help you get there?

- Who are you sharing your success with?

Be as descriptive as possible on your vision of success. Pay attention to what lights you up as you dream of how big and how successful you want to be.

Sometimes, it's helpful to use a vision board. Cut out images from magazines and add inspiring quotes. You can even include a photo of a real person who is living your dream. It gets very exciting when you can bring them into your plan. I have put people I admire on my board, and worked up the courage to let them know. They've become mentors and friends of mine for life.

Dream BIG

Dan Sullivan, a leading sales and leadership coach, talks about making the goal for your business a "10x goal". For example, if you're selling $100,000, imagine selling $1 million. If you're selling $1 million, set your sights on $10 million.

The reason Dan Sullivan recommends expressing your goal by 10x rather than anything less is compelling.

> *"When you set your sights on the goal of a 10x bigger future, something immediately happens to your thinking, your innovation, your decision-making, your communication, and your action."*
> *~ Dan Sullivan*

According to Sullivan, incremental goals (like 2x) simply don't engage people the same way intellectually or emotionally.

I had my suspicions about this, so I asked a number of travel professionals: "What would it feel like to do 10x the sales volume that you're doing right now?".

Some would smile, while others would laugh nervously. Not once with all the advisors I asked did anyone say, "I could *never* achieve that". In other words, the ability to visualize yourself as extraordinary is both possible and *powerful*. And with that, you know deep down that if you had the resources, access to the right people, and the necessary skills, *you can do anything.*

A Mindset Shift of seeing yourself as the best version of yourself, played out in the world, has an ironic sense of calm. It's like saying to yourself, *"Of course! That's the way it should be".*

> *"If you want the best the world has to offer, offer the world your best."*
> ~ **Neale Donald Walsch**

Now, consider the goal you set for yourself and multiply it by ten. Yes it *is* possible! Take a moment to let this sink in: *you've got this.*

> *"Nothing is impossible. The word itself says, 'I'm Possible'."*
> ~ **Audrey Hepburn**

Purpose

The next critical aspect of the Mindset Shift is knowing your purpose and how it impacts the way you serve others.

Mark Twain said, *"The two most important days in your life are the day you are born and the day you find out why."*

Finding your purpose starts with finding your "why" Thanks to Simon Sinek, we have learned that, *"People don't buy what you do; they buy why you do it."*

Let's go back to that day you decided to become a travel advisor. Why did you decide to join the industry?

Perhaps you were passionate about traveling the globe. Maybe you loved cruising, or finding those off the beaten path getaways, and wanted to share your experiences with others so that they could experience the same joy. These are all very good reasons to be in this business.

However, the answer to your "why" that will give clarity for yourself is much deeper than that. **It's about moving from relying on your passion and now determining and being fuelled by your very unique purpose.**

A Mindset Shift is knowing your purpose and operating from a place where fulfilling it becomes all that matters.

It's easy to confuse passion and purpose. In fact, people use

Passion	Purpose
Common to the travel industry	Unique to you
You have many passions	You only have one purpose
Passion comes and goes throughout your life	Purpose never leaves you, from early childhood to the last days of your life
You drop passion when times get tough	You engage your gift of purpose even more when times get tough
You're only willing to do some things	You're willing to do whatever it takes

them interchangeably. However, they are quite different.

Knowing your purpose creates awareness that you were born to do your travel business in a way that is *completely unique to you*. This clarity makes it easier for you to say "yes" to opportunities and "no" to the things that don't matter. It puts an end to comparison with others in the industry and sets you apart from everyone else.

The travel industry is a very crowded space. You need to *stand out* so that the people who need you most can find you. When you are fulfilling your life's purpose as an advisor, the people who need you are drawn to that uniqueness.

You will never compete with others because, like you, they have their own purpose and you have yours. Your purpose ends the comparison of yourself to others. You will run your own race.

Once you discover your purpose, you will measure your days against what you did to fulfil it. If your purpose is to teach, then you will teach your clients. If your purpose is to help people, then your travel business will be full of examples of the extraordinary ways in which you've helped them.

I track my purpose with a jar of marbles. I learned this simple exercise from leadership expert Ken Blanchard, who wrote *The One Minute Manager*, and others. He suggested that every time you make a difference in someone's life, move a paper clip from one jar to the next as a visual reminder to help others.

To support my purpose, I move a marble from one jar to another as a visual cue that I'm making a difference, one person at a time. If I lose my way and get caught up in worry, stress, or the things that seem larger than life in the moment (but really aren't), I figure out a way to move a marble.

So, how do you find your purpose? Consider these five things:

1. **What have people been saying about you your entire life?**
Write a list of words, phrases, and compliments you've heard over the years. Write down three words that come to mind. If you're not sure, take a quick survey. You'll be surprised by how people from completely different parts of your life will use similar words to describe you.

2. **What is something that comes easily to you that other people struggle with?**
Some people would rather eat broken glass than speak in public. Others were born with a microphone in their hand. Some advisors will spend hours researching hundreds of hotel options, while others can make a quick judgment call and create a satisfied customer 99% of the time. What do people come to you for help with that others see as a challenge?

3. **The Easy A or the Gifted Street Smarts.**
Think back to school subjects. Which classes were your easy As? For some, your purpose revealed itself at an early age in the subjects you gravitated toward in school. For others, your gifts did not reveal themselves in your grades. Is there anything you're doing now that would surprise your teachers? Often, you read about CEOs and successful entrepreneurs who barely got by in school. They found a life skill

that was unique, and married it with a crowd of people who needed it.

4 **What were you doing the last time you lost track of time?**
Notice the types of activities that never get bumped from the calendar. Conversely, what would you love to get out of doing if you could? Fulfilling your purpose can mean saying "no" to things you have no business doing.

5 **What do clients most often say about you?**
Do your testimonials have a theme? Notice what they are consistently praising you for. The common theme may surprise you.

Here is a story on how I found my 'why'. Early on in my leadership career, I was in a meeting with my boss, discussing how we could improve our sales programs. I said, "I just had an **epiphany**", he said, "You say that word a lot". We had a good chuckle, as it was an odd word to come up so often.

I hadn't noticed until he pointed it out. I remember thinking, *he's right; I do use that word a lot*. Later that day, the next day, and the day after, I had to fight the urge to say the word 'epiphany'.

I started using different words such as, 'a-ha', 'bumped my head', 'ideation', 'insights', 'breakthrough thought', 'next level', and so on. Now, I must have over a hundred ways to describe the moment when I identify a new way of thinking about something.

Later, while working with Simon Sinek's course 'Finding Your Why' (which I highly recommend), I realized that the reason I was always using the word 'epiphany' is that I live for 'a-ha' moments. My why is finding insights, and sharing them with others to help them grow.

I discovered my 'why' from a casual observation that, under any other circumstances, would not have been memorable. Sometimes finding your 'why' comes down to the simple things you enjoy most.

 ## Service

The final step in the Mindset Shift is about your service proposition and what it means to you and your clients. Your service beliefs, attitude, and actions will determine the trajectory of your entire travel business.

When you are appreciated, valued, and known for making a difference, you feel uplifted and energized. When you feel the opposite — under-appreciated, undervalued, and overwhelmed — it can be exhausting. Over time, it leads to burnout.

There are three key opportunities for standing out when it comes to service.

First, decide *who* you are providing service to. There is a difference between clients who like you and those who become raving fans. Raving fans appreciate your unique ability so much that they would never go anywhere else. In other words, you are truly *their* travel advisor.

Take a moment to think about what your best clients have in common. Over time, you will be able to pick your fans out of a crowded room — literally.

When I was a district sales manager, representing Princess Cruises at a multiple cruise line event, I'd know if we were going to have a successful show based on the people in the room. A Princess fan has a characteristic I could pick out in a crowd. After 17 years of meeting loyal Captain's Circle members, I was able to recognize them almost without speaking.

Who is in your crowd? When you meet someone new and after a short conversation they ask you about travel, does their personality cause you to light up with excitement, or does your mind go to all the reasons it may be hard to take on this client? Taking a position on *who* you serve is central to the Mindset Shift. Everything in your business flows from the decision on *who* you serve.

When you stack the deck in your favor and decide to only work with people who appreciate you, life takes on more meaning and purpose.

My daughter Gillian calls this "loving my odds". When her husband, two children, her dad, and I are gathered around a table, she'll say, *"I love my odds here"*. With five people who love her more than anyone else in the world within hugging distance, she can't go wrong.

In your business, a Mindset Shift on service is about loving your odds and only working with people who appreciate you and your service. This means letting go of the people who switch agents to save 50 dollars. Instead, focus on building the experiences of a lifetime for those who care about you, and be intentional about finding more clients just like them.

The second element of the service proposition is about *how* you serve your clients in order to retain them. The goal is to retain customers for life. Your service proposition should be delivered consistently, have your signature all over it, and be clear about your customer retention objectives. An example of a service proposition might be: "I promise to treat your vacation as if it were my own so that you'll book with me again."

You may think it requires a tremendous effort to retain clients for life. In fact, it does require you to deliver on all your promises. There is no getting away from the diligence required to provide excellent customer service. The good news is that, over time, you will get better and better at your service delivery.

However, service delivery *alone* is not the answer to

establishing repeat clients. In fact, suppliers consistently report on the shocking rate at which clients change agencies. According to multiple customer retention studies across a wide spectrum of industries, the number one reason people leave is that they feel *unappreciated*.

Vicki Freed, Senior Vice President of Royal Caribbean, saw this trend in their bookings. When she probed further, she discovered that clients didn't leave their agent because they were unhappy, or that they found a better deal elsewhere. They left because they felt their agent seemed *indifferent* to whether they booked with them again or not. Now, when Vicki addresses agents, she implores them to make clients feel appreciated.

> *"People will forget what you said, people will forget what you did, but people will never forget how you made them feel."*
>
> *~ Maya Angelou*

The last element of the service proposition is knowing your value and being willing to charge for it. You'll find that your very best customers are those who recognize your value and your extraordinary service and are willing to pay for it.

For years, travel advisors have struggled with fees — whether to charge them, how to charge them, and when they should be included.

If you've never charged fees before, and you're worried that clients won't pay them, or that you'll lose clients if you start charging fees, you're in good company. It's completely reasonable to struggle with this. After all, you've worked hard to find clients, especially good ones. It may seem counterintuitive to charge them.

First, it's important to understand the difference between a transaction you conduct, such as issuing a ticket, and a consultation fee. A service fee compensates you for that transaction, especially on low or non-commissionable products. Set a fee structure that is consistent and transparent. A professional or consultation fee is what a client pays you for your research, knowledge, and advice.

There are several very good reasons for charging consultation fees, including your financial well-being, screening out shoppers, and effective time management, to name a few. The one that has the greatest impact for me is that our commitment follows our money. This is commonly referred to as 'having skin in the game'.

Consider this example from an advisor I met a few years ago, who was new to the industry.

Samantha entered the travel business later in life. She had a successful career in the food industry as a broker of Italian fine foods. In her role, she traveled to Italy six times a year or more, and became an expert in the best that Italy had to offer in food, wine, and places to stay. Family and friends were asking her for advice about traveling to Italy so often that she decided to become an agent. She started part time by putting tours together. After a few months and several successful tours, she left her six-figure job to become a full-time travel advisor.

While she was thrilled to be in the travel industry, she was in for a shock at how much she was expected to do for so little money. Her biggest frustration was in sharing her hard-earned expertise, only to have the client switch agents, armed with all of her knowledge.

In her short time in the industry, she had already learned a valuable lesson. There would always be people who needed her knowledge and expertise. Finding new leads was not her issue. The tricky part was not giving it away for free, and finding those who were willing to pay for her service.

It took tremendous courage for Samantha to start charging a service fee. She suffered with the imposter syndrome — others who were far more experienced in travel weren't charging fees, what made her think she could?

However, based on advice from her host agency, and following the example of advisors she held in the highest regard who were successfully charging fees, she decided to try it.

For thirty days, she responded to every request with a simple statement on her email reply:

"I'd be happy to share my insights that will help you have a *trip of a lifetime to Italy*. All your questions will be answered! I have a $200 consulting fee. If this is agreeable to you, please jump on my calendar at a time that suits you best."

While she did lose a few people, which was hard so early in her business, what surprised her was the response by serious prospects. Not only did they not blink an eye at paying the fee, they stopped going elsewhere with their booking. They knew the value of getting answers to their questions and appreciated her expertise. The difference was they now had their own financial motivation to keep the booking with her. People follow their money.

Overnight, her business became a lot more fun and profitable!

You may find it's better to introduce the fee after a warm introductory conversation, rather than an auto-responder. However, the interesting insight from Samantha was that she put her consultation fee up front, and serious prospects did not blink an eye.

The challenge with bringing up fees after a conversation is that you tend to lose your nerve — especially if you really like the client. Agents have a harder time charging fees to people they like. The irony is, those who like you are the most willing to pay you. Take the money, as it allows you to do *more* for them.

Once you make the shift to understanding that a consultation fee is an acknowledgement of your professional value *and* gives the customer a financial reason to stay with you, it allows you to deliver the kind of service worthy of the fee. It guides your choices of who you work with. It also becomes highly motivating to go and do the work when you know your client is *all in*.

A Final Word on Mindset:
The Decision to Face Your Fears and Do It Anyway

A Mindset Shift is far greater than a goal. It's about achieving your life's ambition. It's bottled up inside of you and waiting to get out! You now have a choice: to remain where you are on your journey, or to rise to where you've *always wanted to go*.

I know that you might be saying to yourself, *"Yes, BUT..."* We all get stifled by the big BUT. BUT takes many shapes and sizes.

- Fear of setbacks: "Oh, I could never achieve it now that the world is on hold."

- Fear of skill gaps: "Oh, I don't know how to do that."

- Fear of opinions: "What will people say?"

- Fear of success: "How will I manage the rest of my life if this really takes off?"

Fear can hold you back for a very long time. We get stifled by the fear of what others will think. After all, going after what you really want requires you to do things that will make you stand out and yet it's been ingrained in us to "fit in".

I remember getting the lead in the school play when I was nine years old. To celebrate, my mom bought me a new pair of sandals to wear to opening night. They were white with a shiny buckle, and they had a high heel! It was only about half an inch high, but it made me feel so grown up. I loved the way the heels clicked when I walked.

I was climbing up a set of stairs to the school theater, glancing down proudly at the music coming from my feet, when I noticed a few girls looking up at me and whispering amongst themselves.

Suddenly, my euphoria turned to embarrassment. *Do they think I'm showing off? Nobody my age wears shoes like these. I wish I was more like them.* I felt the kind of rejection that swells well beyond wearing a pair of shoes.

I was about to put my shoes away for good when my mom gave me some advice that I carry with me to this day.

"You've been given an incredible gift. Use your gifts to rise above everything. Your star will shine bright and be a light to others. Don't listen to those who might criticize. ***Do it for the people who need you to go first."***

Put yourself outside your comfort zone. Do it for yourself, because it will help you grow and reach your dreams. Do it for others who will grow too, inspired by your courage of going first. Face your fears and do it anyway. It's the only way to truly make a difference in the world.

Going after your ambition — while not the easiest nor the straightest path — is the most important path you will take. In his book, *Turning Pro*, Steven Pressfield writes:

> *"To feel ambition and to act upon it is to embrace the unique calling of our souls. Not to act upon that ambition is to turn our backs on ourselves and on the reason for our existence."*

As Dolly Parton says, *"Pour yourself a cup of ambition."* So, go for it!

Chapter Summary
Mindset Shift

1. Mindset shift is a choice. However, unless you support that choice with concrete steps, decision becomes indecision, and you can wallow for a long time.

2. A Mindset Shift has everything you need to see this big idea through. It mobilizes thoughts into beliefs, beliefs into action, and action into results.

3. A Mindset Shift is at the intersection of vision, purpose, and service.

4. A Mindset Shift includes a full-blown version of yourself, living out your vision like a motion picture of your dreams.

5. According to Sullivan, incremental goals (like 2x) simply don't engage people the same way intellectually or emotionally. Consider the goal you set for yourself and multiply it by 10.

6. A Mindset Shift is knowing your purpose and operating from a place where fulfilling it becomes all that matters.

7. The final step in the Mindset Shift is about your service proposition and what it means to you and your clients. Your service beliefs, attitude, and

actions will determine the trajectory of your entire travel business.

8 Everything in your business flows from the decision on who you serve.

9 Face your fears and do it anyway. Its the only way to truly make a difference in the world.

Chapter 2

The Customer Shift — Part One

"Sorry, not accepting any new clients." This sign sat on David's desk. He was clearly the busiest advisor in the office. When I was with Princess Cruises, we were visiting top agencies in Toronto, Ontario. While we were waiting to meet with the agency manager, this sight caught my eye. I remember thinking, *How bold! I'd love to know what that's all about.* I was really hoping to catch a moment with this top producer. Rather than blow me off, David waved me over. He couldn't wait to sit down and ask me about the latest Princess news.

When I asked David about the sign, he laughed and said, "I have had it on my desk for years. But in fact, now, it really is true!" He went on to explain how a few years earlier, he found himself dealing with an endless cycle of walk-in clients and tire kickers. Every client seemed to be price-sensitive, ready to jump to any other agent to save a hundred bucks. Worse, shoppers would tap him for his expertise only to turn around and book online. He was becoming frustrated and disillusioned.

David made a decision to start over and try something completely different. He was going to stop going after new customers where he constantly had to prove himself and instead focus solely on clients he had already worked with. After all, they already knew him and appreciated his service.

Although he admitted that he had done little, if anything, to keep in touch with them, he looked into his customer list and highlighted clients he enjoyed working with. At first, he was reluctant to call due to fear of rejection. Deeper still was the nagging fear that he had lost them and that they had booked with someone else.

David pushed through his fears and now became obsessed with earning and keeping the trust of his most valuable clients. If, in fact, he had lost them to another agency, he asked if they would give him an opportunity on their next booking. "Nothing beats the feeling of winning someone back", he said.

The small change that made the biggest difference was taking the energy he had wasted in frustration of trying to go after every new lead and instead putting all that energy into keeping in touch with his past proven clients. Today, he sells well over seven figures and only accepts clients on a referral basis.

A Customer Shift means you stop trying to be 'all things to all people' and instead move towards being '*everything* to one ideal customer at a time'.

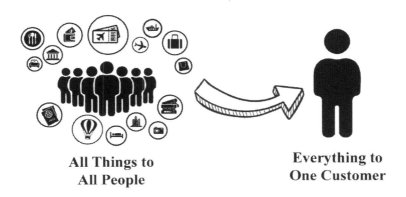

**All Things to
All People**

**Everything to
One Customer**

Think back to when you were in the zone — whether it was your first sale and you did the happy dance, or that feeling when the traveling senior shared a heartfelt "thank you" for what was to be his last cruise. Whether you knew it or not, you were serving your clients, *one important person at a time.*

I like to think of it like this:

Rebuild your database from the bottom of your heart, up.

So what does that mean?

It goes like this. First, you find the perfect customer, the one who makes your heart sing. This gives you the purest motivation to give it your all. Then, you give it your all — you go above and beyond, including that thing you do which makes you feel like you're fulfilling your purpose.

The result is that your customer tells everyone how much they *love* what you do for them. You, in turn, look for other similar customers who would benefit the most from your "everything". It's a constant refining and renewing of doing the right things and finding the right people.

 It doesn't mean you have to go as far as David did and never accept a walk-in or an online request. It means figuring out who brings out the *best* in you, and finding more clients just like them. Over time, you'll find that your service proposition is strongest for a certain type of customer and working with them becomes your competitive advantage.

Ideally, you want a list of between 250 and 500 warm prospects (the number varies depending on your revenue goals) in your database that you reach out to several times a year. When you do service them, you give it everything you've got, one important customer at a time.

Attracting More Customers: Your Customer Avatar
The payoff comes when you take everything you've learned from your "one customer" approach, and apply it to your marketing. This "one customer" is called your customer avatar.

A customer avatar exemplifies your ideals, advocates on your behalf, and serves as the leverage that opens doors to more business.

⬤ Exemplify

An avatar is a person within your network or customer base who **exemplifies** everything you want in a client. They enjoy travel the way you believe travel should be enjoyed. They value your efforts. They are a joy to work with and make you want to do your best work. They don't flinch on price because they understand that, while traveling well costs more, it's worth it. Identifying an avatar who exemplifies everything you're looking for in a client is the key to finding more clients *just like them.*

Advocate

The second characteristic of your avatar is that they
advocate on your behalf. They are your raving fans. They
can't say enough about how wonderful you are to anyone
who even mentions travel. They are your strongest source of
referrals. I had an advisor share with me that she could trace
back over one million dollars in revenue to a single client!

Leverage

The third quality of your avatar is that they provide
important **leverage** to help grow and scale your business.

The travel industry is massive in scope. It's a daily challenge
deciding on what training to take, which suppliers to lean
into, and what technology tools to improve on. Leveraging
your avatar means literally using their needs and desires as
a lens for everything you do.

The Tale of Two Advisors

To demonstrate the power of leveraging your avatar, we
have a tale of two advisors. Meet **Lucy Leverage** and **Sally
Squirrel**.

Lucy Leverage entered the industry as a cruise enthusiast.
She had cruised on a few cruise lines, including Princess.
She was an "almost empty nester," and her circle of

influence was in a similar life stage.

She decided to focus on Princess because she was already familiar with the product and they had a sales academy, so she could learn how to sell it. Lucy was passionate in helping families who put a high value on educational and enriching vacations.

Lucy Leverage soon became a Princess commodore specializing in Alaskan and European cruise tours for families. Within 18 months, she was selling $100,000 per month.

Sally Squirrel started with an equally impressive travel background. She was a passionate traveler. She and her husband had a goal to "plant their flag" on every continent before they were 65.

To begin with, Sally Squirrel couldn't get enough of every travel supplier training event. She started with the Princess Academy, followed by Sandals, Crystal, Club Med, and more. Before too long, Sally's enthusiasm was dwindling. She became overwhelmed by how much there was to learn. Her prospecting and selling stalled, and Sally eventually gave up. She squirrelled off to another opportunity.

Leveraging your avatar to determine your training plan will increase your focus and allow you to learn a vast amount of knowledge in a short period of time. You can convert that knowledge directly into growing more customers. Be like

Lucy Leverage, not like Sally Squirrel.

The Avatar of the Future: Attracting New Clients

Avatars should be within the target market you are most interested in growing. Even if you have never sold to anyone in it. Perhaps you want to sell to more luxury clients or high-end villas. You may not know anyone in that market, and that's okay. An avatar can be someone that you *want* to work with. For example, if you're interested in specializing in expedition cruises but have yet to sell one, you can create a fictional expedition avatar.

Do your homework first, though. Interview clients who have been there. If you still don't know anyone, ask other advisors and suppliers for specific client feedback. Get onto websites and look for authentic testimonials. Read industry reports such as Cruise Industry News Annual Expedition Report and Travel Market Report's *Expedition Cruise Outlook*. You will find these reports are chock full of important data and testimonials from top selling advisors who already have an impressive book of business selling expeditions.

The goal is to create a complete profile of your expedition avatar in detail, including age, income, education, interests, etc. Understanding everything about your avatar will help you create content, host events, and write newsletters that are targeted at them. Even if you have never sold to a single customer, this process will make these coveted clients feel like you're speaking directly to them.

Remember, there has to be a first time for everything. These are all brave steps forward! In growing your business the way you want it to grow, and working with clients you love to serve. This process will take time to perfect but don't use lack of experience as a reason to hold you back from reaching your goal.

How to Choose Your First A-lister: Your Ideal Client

Whether you're starting out in a new market, building clients, or shifting your focus, it is essential that you work with people who value what you have to offer. Consider these three areas as a starting point for choosing your avatar: life stage, travel style, and milestones.

 Life Stage.

The life stages of Generation Z, Gen Y, Millennial, Gen X, and Baby Boomers are theoretically each a generation apart. Because of these large gaps, and because we most effectively sell what we know from firsthand experience, it's only natural and advisable to focus on your own age bracket. If you're in the young family stage, for instance, you know traveling with children like the back of your hand.

 Travel Style.

Shifting to a travel lifestyle generally means shifting to luxury or ultra-luxury travel. There are many benefits from shifting up market, including selling higher-priced products that yield higher commissions, increased travel frequency and access into a network of affluent friends.

However, be sure to shift to a luxury level you're already comfortable and familiar with yourself. If you can't imagine spending $30,000 a night on a villa, then it's almost impossible to move comfortably among people who think nothing of it. A top-selling luxury advisor once said to me, "Ultra-luxury clients test you to ensure you understand their lifestyle".

Start your luxury shift where you feel the greatest *conviction*. Selling slightly outside your comfort zone is a *must*. Selling way outside your comfort zone, however, won't resonate with the client.

 Milestones.

A good way to narrow your focus is to work with everyone reaching a milestone, such as a 50th birthday, retirement, or 25th wedding anniversary. Each of these milestones has significant meaning in our lives. Adding a milestone to your avatar helps give more definition to what matters most about each vacation.

Some milestones, such as a 50th birthday, may even mean multiple trips. It could be a mother-daughter trip, a girlfriend getaway, or a special multigenerational family trip.

What if I Have More Than One Avatar?

Most of us struggle with this concept: I can't decide on just one area of interest! *"I love families, but I also love working with empty nesters." "I sell a lot of all-inclusive beach vacations and cruises, but I want to shift to river cruising."*

A one-customer-at-a-time approach works best if you choose a single avatar. The reason you may be stuck at a current revenue level, burnt out, or tired is that you're being pulled in too many directions. Choosing more than one avatar and the necessary marketing and messaging that goes along with it can become overwhelming and confusing very quickly. While you should **sell** to a wide array of customers, it is best practice to only market to one.

> *"If you chase two rabbits, you will lose them both."*
>
> *~ **Leonard Nimoy***

The good news is that by narrowing your focus to one customer at a time you will uncover important *adjacent* market opportunities. Consumers have a variety of interests and can belong to several segments at the same time. For example, a couple can be ultra-luxury for their own travel but move to a contemporary market when taking their children and grandchildren on a multigenerational trip.

Here are examples of how choosing one avatar can open up an entirely new market:

Avatar	Adjacent Market Opportunity
Bride	Mother of the bride
Golfer	A group to the British Open
50th birthday	Girlfriend getaway
Girlfriend getaway	Multi-gen cruise
Wine connoisseur	Wine groups

Remember, your ideal customer will bring others to you. Having a single message cuts through the clutter and will ring true if you solve the unique problems of a single client.

Positioning Yourself as Indispensable

To become "my" travel advisor, beyond your current client list, you need to become indispensable. You need to do things for clients that are so important, so endearing and make such a difference to their vacation experience that they cannot imagine booking travel without you. As my favorite business quote of all time says:

"Whatever you do, do it well. Do it so well when people see you do it they will want to come back and see you do it again and they will want to bring others and show them how well you do what you do."

~ Walt Disney

Once you *are* indispensable, you need to communicate *how* you are indispensable.

While it can be about those heroic things you do for clients, more often, being indispensable comes from demonstrating a high level of excellence in all the little things that matter when booking a trip.

Take a blank sheet of paper. On one side, write down **"All the Things I Do."** On the other side, write down, **"That Thing I Do"** that makes you special.

Notice what stands out for you. *That thing you do* goes back to your purpose. The way in which you serve people is completely unique to you. You've been doing it your entire life. Even when doing the everyday tasks of your job, your gifts will shine through.

If you're stuck, think back to specific feedback from clients, teachers, and family.

Start with three words that describe you. For example, my entire life, the word "enthusiasm" has followed me. Over time, I've come to realize that empathy and grit are at the core of "that thing that I do" for the people I serve.

I have created this tagline for my coaching business: *"Lead with enthusiasm, empathy, and grit every day!"* I don't read it like a script, but I try my best to live up to it and deliver upon it everyday.

Use this exercise to create your own positioning statement that lets people know what makes you unique, and what they can expect when they work and book with you.

Chapter Summary
Customer Shift — Part One

1. Rebuild your database from the bottom of your heart — up!

2. The key to a successful travel business is the consistent refining of doing the right things and finding the right people.

3. It means figuring out who brings out the best in you and finding more clients just like them.

4. An avatar is a customer who exemplifies your ideals, advocates on your behalf, and serves as the leverage that opens doors to more business.

5. Leveraging your Avatar means using their needs and desires as a lens for everything you do.

6. Leveraging your avatar to determine your training plan will increase your focus and allow you to learn a vast amount of knowledge in the shortest time.

7. Be like Lucy Leverage and not Sally Squirrel.

8. Avatars should be within the target market you are most interested in growing. Even if you have never sold to anyone in it.

9 Selling slightly outside your comfort zone is a must. Selling way outside your comfort zone, however, will not resonate with the client.

10 Consider these three areas as a starting point for choosing your avatar: life stage, travel style, and milestones.

11 While you should sell to a wide array of customers, it's a best practice to only market to one.

12 To become "my" travel advisor beyond your current client list, you need to become indispensable.

Chapter 3

The Customer Shift — Part Two

Your Marketing Plan

Now that you've narrowed the focus on your customer avatar, it's time to roll up your sleeves and create a marketing plan that will allow you to grow a steady stream of ideal clients.

A marketing plan, at its very basic level, includes the who, what, where, when and why of your travel business. It is a framework for you to promote the right products, at the right price, at the most likely time and place to capture the interests of your target market.

There are aspects of a plan that are fluid and constantly changing, such as the products you sell, and the available offers. But there's an important foundation to a plan that *never* changes: your *purpose* and *who you want to serve*.

It's like the foundation of a house. If the bones are right, you can do miracles with the décor. If the bones are wrong, no amount of paint can make up for a bad layout.

Too often, you can be overwhelmed by "promotion commotion". You may have the best deals and unlimited offers, but without a solid foundation of good clients and an effective means of reaching them, it's all wasted.

Create a framework for your marketing that's centered on "why". Consider your purpose and who you want to serve, then your business will become much less chaotic. Deciding what to promote becomes much easier. Closing ratios improve, and commissions increase.

Who (Your Avatar)

We've established that your avatar is your ideal customer. He or she is the person who would most likely rave about you, and vice versa. When it comes to your marketing plan, your avatar will be the person you communicate with at every level.

From website content to what products you choose to promote, your avatar is the "who" in your marketing plan.

Keep in mind that you're only attracting *the very best* clients for your business. They, in turn, will bring their friends. The key to marketing is to start small. Seth Godin refers to this as your *"minimum viable audience",* in other words, who would care deeply if you didn't show up? Write your content directly at them.

Content marketing is like taking a conversation with your avatar public. Everything you create — from your website to your newsletter — needs to be consistently positioned with your avatar in mind. From the products you sell to the travel tips you provide, your content needs to show off your expertise and how you solve your client's problems and concerns. Chances are, if one ideal client has an issue, it is likely that many others will as well. The sign on your agency door says that you are 'here to help'.

"What helps people, helps business."

~ Leo Burnett

Consider Martha, a top-selling advisor from Vancouver. She started working as a travel advisor fifteen years ago, selling mostly cruises. Three years ago, she took her first river cruise, and she was hooked! She loved the smaller ship, the relaxed ambiance, and the extensive tours.

As soon as she arrived on the ship, however, she realized her first mistake — she had packed all wrong! As an avid cruiser, she hadn't taken the time to realize that river cruising is a lot more relaxed. She ended up wearing the same outfit on three of the seven nights and returned home with a suitcase full of unworn dresses.

When she got back to work, she immediately shifted from a broad focus on cruisers in general, to a targeted focus on empty nesters taking their first river cruise.

As she dove in with this new market, she found herself re-telling the packing story over and over with clients. *"When it comes to packing, think touring — not cruising. Leave your fancy dresses at home!"*

She got asked about packing so often, she decided to make a YouTube video: "How to Pack for a River Cruise." The video went viral with over 30,000 views, and it was a boon to her travel business. She now has first-time river cruise clients from all over North America. Her simple strategy of answering a frequently asked question to her closest clients attracted an entirely new market of first-time river cruisers.

What You Sell

After you're clear on who you sell to, it's time to make a declaration on **what** you sell. Your sales are an endorsement of your expertise. **What** you sell communicates to travellers what you believe in.

Consider the spectrum of travel products between low-priced and high-priced, low complexity and high complexity. Don't settle for what you know. Sell for what you love and what you want to be known for.

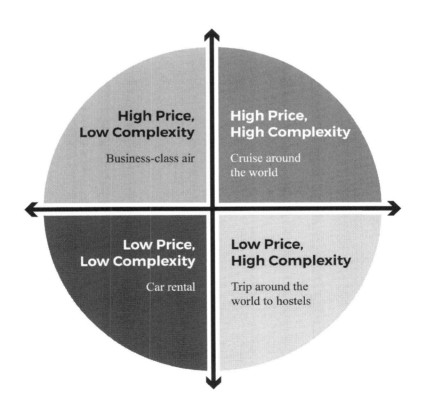

Low price, low complexity products, such as air tickets and car rentals, are simple to book and harder for an advisor to add value to. Therefore, most customers will book them online.

A trip around the world using hostels is **low price-high complexity.** At $30 a night, the commission is practically nonexistent, compared to the effort.

High price, low complexity products such as business class air are important components to add to every booking. Clients will be inclined to think they can book those for themselves. However, it enhances your positioning as the expert on their booking by taking on that segment.

High price, high complexity is the sweet spot for travel advisors. Cruises, tours, and multi-destination stays are examples that fall within this space. The more complex the vacation, the lower the competition and the higher your value is to the client.

Where would you put yourself and the clients you serve on that graph?

Bundling Products Together

Let's consider the benefit of combining quadrant one — high price, low complexity with quadrant two, high-price, high complexity.

When you add components (including airfare, train tickets, experiences, attractions, and insurance) to a cruise or land package, you're creating a completely unique experience. The more *complex* you can make a vacation by pulling all of the segments together into a bundle, the more you will *stand out* in that upper quadrant. You may not want to book someone's air or train tickets for little or no commission. Often, the clients will be comfortable booking their own. However, adding components is not strictly about the commission.

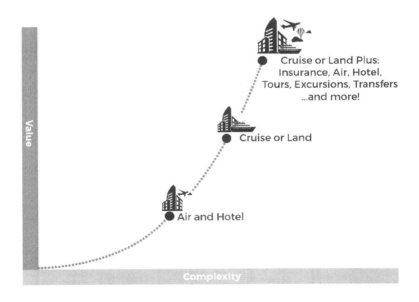

The point of bundling is that when you include air, hotels, and other add-ons , you bring *every* component under your watchful eye. You are now the expert in the client's vacation, doing what you do best!

Secondly, these travel bundles become more difficult to price match. Clients can become distracted when they see their cruise or all inclusive vacation advertised online for a much lower rate. Bundling prevents this distraction. Even adding something such as a simple transfer or excursion helps to create a distinction.

And finally, the more components you add to a booking, the greater the commitment by the client. They begin to look forward to the trip because they can visualize it, every step of the way. Build up the anticipation with photos and details that they can put on their fridge, or add excitement on a travel app!

The goal is to create an uncrowded market segment by creating signature vacations that are not available through any other travel advisor.

However, a word of caution on consistency. It's important that you use the same add ons every time. For example, add a hotel stay prior to every cruise, but use the same hotel. Add a transfer to every booking, but use the same transfer company. Add a private excursion in Tuscany, using the same tour company. In other words, create vacations that are unique in the customers eyes, but highly familiar in yours. Find suppliers that are your go-to for add ons so that you're not re-inventing every time. Which leads to the next point.

What You Sell: A Core List of Suppliers

In order to service all of a customer's travel needs, every

travel advisor must establish a *small* list of preferred partners within a slightly broader range of suppliers. Most consortia and franchises have a list of preferred suppliers. They're well worth supporting due to the commercial terms that have been negotiated on your behalf. However, as an advisor, it's in your best interest to narrow the list even further.

When choosing your partners, start with just *one* from the list. Select a single supplier that reflects the excellence you desire for your own personal brand and is a perfect match for your avatar. Often it's the brand you choose for your own personal vacations, but sometimes it's the supplier that is easiest to do business with or the one that clients ask for most often in your market.

Having a go-to preferred supplier has many benefits. Much of your effort will be on learning, promoting, and selling their brand, which will deepen your expertise and efficiency. Clients will single you out because of your knowledge for the brand. Your sales will grow and so will your industry recognition. In return for sales volume, you will find that this preferred partner will promptly answer all of your questions, and be a lifeline of support when things go off the rails.

Similar to choosing one avatar, choosing a single top supplier will open doors to creating a preferred relationship with "adjacent" top suppliers. Suppliers are keenly aware of the other suppliers you are selling. If you're well known for selling luxury brands, other luxury brands will come calling.

Ultimately, it's not possible to do all of your business with a single supplier brand. However, it's reasonable to do 80% of your business with 20% of the suppliers on your list. In fact, most agents can do a meaningful level of sales across four or five key brands. Your "core four" or "friendly five" suppliers ultimately become those that you do the majority of your business with.

When and Where You Sell: The Drum beat of Your Marketing Plan

The annual calendar has a natural rhythm that creates travel patterns. Since childhood, those travel patterns have been deeply etched into our lives.

As a child, my family grew up going on summer holidays every year. As a parent with my own family, like clockwork we have carried on the tradition by booking trips from June to September.

When cold weather creeps across the Northern United States and Canada, snowbirds flock south to warm destinations. In January, right after we have all spent special family time celebrating Christmas together, many of us start making travel plans for the upcoming year. In fact, cruise lines book more cruises in January (during wave season) than in any other month.

Similarly, destinations around the world have different peak traveling periods. In the South Pacific, people enjoy their summer while we're having winter, therefore January through April is an ideal time to travel there. Europe is perfect for families in the summer and through the fall for retirees. Alaska is ideal during the summer months and offers prime wildlife viewing in May and features the breathtaking autumn colours in September.

Set your business up for success by planning around calendar trends accordingly. Work with your core partners to find out what the best time to promote their brand is. For example, Princess has a "sailing and mailing" calendar that matches the best time to promote products based on when the ships sail.

River cruise lines with smaller ships and limited capacities sell out much faster — often more than a year in advance. Destinations like Provence in France, with their lavender in full bloom for only 2 weeks in early July, are very popular itineraries with limited capacity. It's essential to know and communicate to your prospect and clients the peak selling periods of the most popular destinations they want to travel to.

Enter each of these key trends into a calendar and create your marketing plan around when the best time is to promote them. For example:

When you settle into an annual pattern, it creates efficiencies in your travel business. It allows you to book suppliers well in advance for travel shows, and take advantage of any early booking discounts for your clients.

Promotions Plan with Destinations	
Month	**Destination**
January	Alaska
February	Europe
March	River cruises
April	Multi-generation family
May	World cruises
June	Cruising
July	Hawaii/Caribbean
August	Family
September	Europe
October	Exotic
November	Expedition
December	New ships

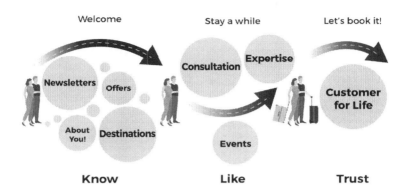

Welcome   Stay a while   Let's book it!

Know   Like   Trust

Your Marketing Tool Kit

In order to attract new A-list clients, you need to be *easy to find*. You require a highly visible online presence that creates the right impression 52 weeks a year, so that when the time is right, you're the first person they contact.

You also need to go and *find* your ideal clients through networking, referrals, and events. This section covers all of the marketing vehicles that will help you attract and retain ideal clients, including your website, newsletters, social media, and virtual events.

Let's dig into an overview of the marketing tools that will help you attract and retain a fabulous client base. Some of these you'll need to build, and others will be provided for you by your organization. Remember, whether you're building your business, rebranding your business, or joining a marketing machine, nobody can sell YOU like you can.

Marketing YOU — Welcome Home!

Last year, I attended a celebration of life for a dear family friend who passed away just shy of his 100th birthday. The event took place at the Italian Cultural Center in Vancouver, a local venue which had been Guido's gathering place for much of his life. After a lavish dinner-sized lunch and heartfelt speeches, I got up to stretch my legs.

The long, sweeping hallways were adorned with smiling photos of past presidents dating back to the early 1950s. There were pictures of hundreds of happy brides and grooms saying their vows, babies in their christening gowns, and other milestone tributes that filled these rooms over the years.

As I looked into the common room, I observed a dozen seniors playing cards, chatting the afternoon away in Italian and sharing stories. I couldn't understand a word of their conversation, but I could feel the deep connection that they had. In that moment, I felt a longing to belong. I don't live close by and I am not Italian, but I wondered how I could find my way into this warm and welcoming community.

Your business community needs a place to find you. When they do, it needs to be welcoming. They need to see people "just like them" hanging out there, and they need to feel like they belong.

With online marketing, all paths lead to home, and home

is your website. Your website needs to convey a warm welcome for visitors who are dropping by and serve as a gathering place for your members. Your newsletters, social media, videos, and events live within your online community center.

Whether you're running the marketing for a large-scale website, or responsible for representing yourself online, the same principals of creating a warm welcome to your community with a consistent message apply.

Website
Your website is where customers can find *everything* that they need to know about you, your products, and your promotions.

This can be as simple as a one-page landing page, or an "About Me" section on your consortia's website. Or it a can be an elaborate website with an online booking engine. While you can spend $500 or $5,000, the key is to start small. Create a place that directs clients to learn more about you, your services, and your events. The flow is to move visitors to friends, and friends to customers.

The mistake most agents make is that they get carried away creating a complex website that is hard to maintain. It doesn't need to be elaborate, but it does need to convert traffic into warm leads.

Create Your Home Page: Everything a Customer Needs to Know About Working with You

Whether you're starting from scratch or reinventing your business, think about your website as a description of what it's like to work with you. What would you want everyone to know?

- **Who you are** — your positioning statement, your experience, expertise, how you view travel, or a favorite travel quote, for example.

- **Who you serve** — your ideal customer testimonials, photos, and travel stories.

- **Why book with you** — offers, partners, and programs.

- **Where you are** — how to interact with you if you work from home or an office.

- **What's happening** — *Always* have an "upcoming" event. It reduces cold calling and connects you with many prospects at the same time.

- **How clients can reach you** — your contact information.

- **How clients can stay in touch and become friends** — Have them subscribe to your email list to get hot travel tips straight to their inboxes.

- **Fresh content, current photos, and interesting travel tips** — convey how you do travel best!

Consider how you will stop traffic from looking any further to other travel advisors and their websites. People want to be saved from the online search rabbit hole. Include three compelling calls to action: subscribe, contact, and book.

Newsletter

A newsletter is a weekly, bi-weekly, or monthly update on all things travel. It's your take on what your customers need to know. Despite the noise and popularity of social media, communicating with clients *with their permission* in a newsletter is *still* the most effective form of travel marketing. Done well, it's like doing 100 or 1,000 sales calls all at once. It keeps you connected with clients and builds rapport so that when the time is right to call, it will be the warmest call you'll ever make!

Creating your own newsletter can be a fun focus for your entire business.

Theme

Mapping out your newsletter theme will make your life so much easier in the long run.

Set a frequency for your newsletter that is both reasonable and appreciated. Bi-weekly or weekly is sufficient for an exclusive client list, especially if you are adding in regular social posts, and staying in touch with phone calls.

Good marketing is about being in your clients inbox with

Promotions Plan with Destinations and Themes

Month	Destination	Theme
January	Alaska	Escorted Groups
February	Europe	Tuscany Cooking Schools
March	River Cruises	Wine Cruises
April	Multi-generation family	Top Family Activities
May	World Cruises	5 Best Itineraries
June	Cruising	World of Cruising On Sale
July	Hawaii/Caribbean	Unpack the Sun Sale
August	Family	Fall in Love with Travel
September	Europe	Top Spa Retreats
October	Exotic	Romance South Pacific/Tahiti
November	Expedition	Expedition Expert Event
December	New ships	15 New Vessels

the right product, and the right message so that when the time is right, they think of you. Keep it simple, as a majority of the time, clients are making note for future travel.

Calls to Action

When the time is right, it is useful to fill your newsletters with multiple calls to action that will create more enquiries and potential sales. This can include a phone number, a weblink to place a booking, or an invitation to a special event or promotion. The objective here is to deepen clients' interest from *thinking* about travel to *talking* about travel to *booking* travel. All of these tactics create a reason to follow up which in turn leads to greater sales!

It is important to think of creative ways you can get clients to reach out to you. For example, you can create a dedicated e-book with tips and insights about travel, which you can then use as a lead magnet to entice website visitors to subscribe. Contests, community events, and travel giveaways can all generate excitement and interest that can lead to a conversation.

Ultimately, the newsletter itself won't pick people up and drive them into your store. You still have to politely go and get them, so to speak.

But where to start?

Once you send your newsletter, watch for the data that it will generate. Newsletter tracking and e-book downloads will reveal who's visited your website and what they're most interested in. You are like a detective, *looking for clues* from prospects who are "in your store" shopping. They are the ones to follow up with.

With all of these efforts, you will have turned non-existent or cold leads into warm leads! So it is now time to reach out and ask about their travel plans. Not doing so is almost like asking them to go book somewhere else!

Social Media

It is essential to understand the power of social media and how to effectively integrate it into your shift.

I will start with a word of caution. For social media to be effective, it involves a tremendous amount of time and attention — far more than you can ever get a return on, if you're not careful. Fortunately, there are excellent training resources available on how to implement a simple and effective social media campaign. There are also very reasonable services that can assist you with curating content, calendaring, and posting! I prefer to do my own engaging as it feels more authentic, but I know some people who outsource that as well.

In short, it's important to have enough knowledge to understand social media, but it *can't become the job*. You will burn out quickly if you don't create a strong discipline around the hours spent versus the return on your time.

We all know, social media can also be a depressing space. So, before we proceed, take a moment to think about your approach and how you might want to delegate some of this effort in the future. For example, if you can generate a single additional booking per month, that's enough revenue to hire a virtual assistant to execute your social media.

Now, let's look at getting a clear understanding of what you need to know to make your plan effective.

It is reasonable to suggest that social media is now the most powerful marketing media for growing your business. In fact, ninety percent of companies leverage it in their digital strategy. The average consumer spends 2.5 hours a day on social media — and this number is growing with younger audiences. Eighty-one percent of consumers say that digital media has influenced their buying decisions.

Travel is the ideal subject matter for social media content. It has the powerful advantage of being so visually enticing. As they say, a picture is worth a thousand words. It's inspirational and generates well-above-average engagement from audiences.

Social Media Strategy

Similar to your website approach, the purpose of a social media plan is to attract and retain your ideal client for the purpose of doing business with you.

Unlike a website, however, social media moves your business out of your "store". You are now in the community, moving about and sharing your goodness with people who are just like you.

Before going a step further, remember that imaginary but important line of permission marketing that we all know from email marketing. There are stringent rules in place about having a client's permission to email them. The same rules apply to social media, although they are not enforced. It goes against the rules of engagement to *sell* overtly on your social media platform without permission to do so.

And yet, people do it all the time.

Nothing is more of a turnoff than when, as a friend to someone on Facebook, they begin to relentlessly sell things to you that you're not interested in. Without your permission, they in effect changed the dynamics of your friendship. It certainly wasn't the unspoken agreement when you initially became friends. If you step over the line and become too commercial, they will block you and you've lost them altogether.

To be clear, this doesn't mean never sell on social media. It's about striking a balance with the emphasis on helpful content over a commercial message. The occasional too-good-to-be-true offer, special escorted departure, or consumer event, falls into the category of helpful content.

Another way to look at it is, "Join me on my journey" content.

What do I mean by "join me on my journey"? Your friends, customers and circle of influence, care about your journey to becoming their travel advisor. It's like having a backstage pass to your dreams. They are cheering you on! So yes, post that event you worked hard to put together and photos of your team having an amazing time. Post pictures of your best clients enjoying their 30th anniversary. Add social media posts of exotic locales and beautiful quotes that inspire travel. That is engaging content.

Social media is a platform for engaging your following so that they know, like, and trust you. Let people get to know you by sharing your dreams and understanding what you're passionate about. Include photos of you doing what you love in order to build rapport. Finally, provide valuable problem solving tips and sage advice that will build trust.

Your strategy is to build rapport and to move the dialogue to a one-on-one conversation. Take the steps to invite your following to your business page where they will be more open to receiving offers. Be sure to subscribe them to your email, and follow up with a phone call for your most engaged clients.

Here are seven steps to creating a profitable social media plan:

 Get visible on social media with your A-listers.
According to social media expert Koka Sexton, the number-one rule of social selling is, *"Visibility creates opportunity"*.

You need to spend time communicating and being present on social media where your high-value prospects are hanging out. In fact, Google states that 95% of travel purchases start online! Even your most loyal customers start looking long before they reach out to you.

There are multiple social media platforms that include Facebook, Instagram, Twitter, YouTube, LinkedIn, TikTok, and Pinterest. The question to ask yourself is, *"Where do my A-listers hang out?"*.

 Curate high quality content that is eye-catching.
Use beautiful photography that reflects the quality of your work and your view of the way your clients travel. Invest $10 for a professional photo from Shutterstock, Pixaby, Adobe or Canva, or use free sources such as Unsplash — but ALWAYS give photo credit.

Use videos that are short, to the point and well done. It doesn't have to be a studio production, in fact, genuine personalized videos come across very well. However, do make an effort to learn the basics of lighting, lens placement and sound.

 **Create or curate content that solves a problem.** Once you've identified a few problems, begin to create and collect solutions. Become an expert on the problems that most of your A-listers share.

Let's consider five common problems that motivate vacationers to look for solutions via online content:

- **Travel is complex and confusing.** How do I know which is the best cruise for me? Now more than ever, will there be safety protocols in place?
  Solution: Create content to position yourself as the expert in the complexities that clients hadn't even considered.

- **I can't take vacation because I'm too busy at work.**
  Solution: Create content that reminds people of the growing need to find life balance. Mental illness, stress, and burnout are now prevalent in 30% of the workforce.

- **FOMO — Fear of missing out!** I'm afraid I'll book the wrong hotel, resort, or cruise and miss out on the one I should have booked.
  Solution: Create an ongoing tip sheet of mistakes to avoid when booking travel.

- **When is the best time to book?** The most common misperception people have is that it's better to book last minute because they don't fully comprehend the value of booking early.
  Solution: Reinforce early booking *value*, not price. Emphasize that choice, flexibility, options, availability, and overall experience are all much better the earlier you book.

- **How do I make everyone happy when we're traveling in our "bubble"?** I'm traveling with my kids and in-laws, but my husband and I need a break, too!
  Solution: Create content that appeals to solving multigenerational travel challenges, such as babysitting for children or excursions suited to all mobility types.

 Create a social media content calendar.
When it comes to posting your articles or sharing others, it can be very time consuming. It's easy to see why travel agents become overwhelmed with this process.

I suggest creating a simple social media posting calendar and content repository. There are automated apps such as 'Later' that you can load up so that you can schedule the posting dates in advance.

Whether you do it yourself or hire someone, it's

helpful to stockpile content and store useful articles in one place that you can reuse so that posting on social media takes two hours once a week rather than an hour or more everyday.

5 **Follow key influencers.**
Find and follow a few influencers within the segments you want to be famous for. A professional influencer in travel wins or loses their reputation by the content they post. It's easy to spot someone who is in it for the perks. Instead, look for people who are traveling in the same style and interest level that you are recommending for your clients. A safe bet is to follow influencers who are endorsed by companies you trust such as AMA, Seabourn, and Oceania. They can be your eyes and ears "on the ground".

I know advisors who have developed strong collaborations by getting to know reputable influencers. Most influencers have no interest in booking travel, yet they often are asked to make bookings. It can be a win-win relationship that develops over time from mutual trust.

6 **Play the engagement game.**
The social media platform algorithms reward posts that receive high engagement. In order to increase the visibility of your post, engage with your likes and comments. It's helpful to have a support crew of fellow entrepreneurs who also play the engagement

game. Be generous and help others, and they will help you in return. Even a single comment changes the trajectory of the ranking. The more people who see your posts, the greater the impact.

 Move the conversation to email, text, or Zoom. The goal for all social media conversations is to get into a committed relationship with those who want to do business with you.

Use social media in a way that excites people to get in touch with you. Move people from Facebook to email so that you are in a one-on-one conversation, not in a crowd. Ask them to sign up for your newsletter with a convenient opt-in form.

Virtual Events

Prior to the pandemic, virtual events were received with a moderate response. Some advisors found them successful, but the general thought was that nothing could come close to an in-person event for creating excitement and bookings.

Enter the lockdown. Isolation and social distancing, combined with free Zoom for everyone has made the virtual platform a completely acceptable form of consumer event.

Virtual events are a fraction of the cost of in-person events, and without the need to travel, you can book fascinating keynote speakers, create panels of experts, and host a regular travel series with very little logistics and lead-time.

Get busy learning how you can leverage this important new tool. I predict that in some form or another, virtual events will remain very relevant in the future.

To host an effective virtual consumer event, the goal is to set the bar as high as you can without thinking you need to be the next award-winning broadcast. Here are 12 tips for tuning up your virtual consumer event game:

1   **Be riveting and vivacious before you start.**
My mother always said, "People see you before you see them". Enter the virtual meeting room smiling, confident, and excited to greet people.

2   **Stand up! (and put your heels on, if applicable)!**
You create a commanding presence and convey energy when you strike a comfortable, powerful pose.

3   **Light your face well.**
Watch for any glare on the screen.

4   **Consider your background.**
Keep the wall art behind you simple, for instance. Be careful with Zoom backgrounds as, unless they are done on a green screen, they will be blurry the moment you move.

5   **Aim the camera in the upper half of your body with your head in the center of the frame.**

If you are co-hosting, be sure that your screen presence matches so that both of you have the same on-screen profile.

6   **Make Eye Contact.**

Look at the center of the camera, not at your screen. Place a sticky note on the webcam to remind yourself. It feels awkward at first but it's the difference between someone looking straight into your eyes, and looking down at you.

7   **Never let them see you sweat.**

Technology always has its glitches. Chat through the mishaps and make them part of the show.

8   **Lights, camera, and a microphone are must-haves!**

I'm not here to recommend any gear in particular. I did want to mention that I purchased the entry-level of each component, and my sound and picture quality are now noticeably above average. I'm sure I could have spent much more, but at less than $500 total, these components were well worth the investment!

9   **Cut the time in half.**

Virtual attention spans are far shorter than you think. Don't translate an in-person meeting or event at the same ratio as a virtual one. Half the time, or slightly more than half, is about right. Invite people to stay longer if they have time, but keep it to the timing you planned on the agenda.

10 **Engage the audience from the outset with an icebreaker in the chat.**
Getting them used to chatting will keep them conversational throughout.

11 **Break up every 20 minutes with an engaging activity.**
Such as 'your pet show and tell', sharing a favorite travel photo, or finding something red. You can make up whatever game suits your audience.

12 **Use breakout rooms.**
Keep the numbers small and, if possible, assign a facilitator.

This is the perfect time to offer tremendous value to your customers who may not be up to visiting you in person. Share a valuable or meaningful service that shows you care. When the time is right, they will think of you first.

Summary
Your Customer Shift is about moving from trying to be *all things to all people* to being *everything for one*. One perfect avatar will open the opportunity to get your message to thousands of others. Write your newsletter directly to your avatar. Post for them, help them, serve them, and invite

them to your events. When the time is right, they will book with you, you will wow them, and they will book again and again. In turn, they will bring their friends to see you do what you do best!

If there is one area of your travel business that benefits from time, attention, effort, and inspiration, it's marketing.

It may seem arduous at first, even overwhelming. However, once you're set up with a who, what, where, when framework, the heavy lifting is done. From there, small actions done consistently every day will transform your business.

"As a marketer, you have to be the inspiration from inside the company."

~ Ashton Kutcher

Chapter Summary
Customer Shift — Part two

1. Focus your marketing on your purpose and who you want to serve. Your business will become much less chaotic.

2. Content marketing is like taking a conversation with your avatar public. Everything you create — from your website to your newsletter — needs to be consistently positioned with your avatar in mind.

3. **Who**: Your Customer Avatar is your ideal customer.

4. **What**: Your sales are an endorsement of your expertise. What you sell communicates to travellers what you believe in.

5. The more complex the vacation, the lower the competition and the higher your value is to the client.

6. To service all customer travel needs, every advisor must establish a small list of preferred partners.

7. **When** and **Where** you sell is the drumbeat of your marketing plan.

8. The calendar has a natural rhythm to it that creates travel patterns.

It's essential to know and communicate to your avatars the peak selling periods of the most popular destinations they want to travel to.

9. In order to attract A-list clients, you need to be easy to find.

10. You require a highly visible online presence that creates the right impression 52 weeks a year, so that when the time is right, you are the first person they contact.

11. Your website is where customers can find everything that they need to know about you, your products, and your promotions.

12. Create a place that directs clients to learn more about you, your services, and your events. The flow is to move visitors to friends, and friends to customers.

13. Consider how you will stop traffic from looking any further to other travel advisors and their websites. People want to be saved from the online search rabbit hole.

14. Set a frequency for your newsletter that is both reasonable and appreciated.

15. You are like a detective, *looking for clues* from prospects who are "in your store" shopping.

16. In short, it is important to have enough knowledge to understand social media, but it can't become the job!

17. Social media is a platform for engaging followers so they know, like, and trust you.

18. Your friends, customers and circle of influence care about your journey to becoming their travel advisor.

19. The strategy is to move the dialogue from social media into a one-on-one conversation.

20. Whether you do it yourself or hire someone, it is helpful to stockpile useful articles in one place.

21. Virtual events are a fraction of the cost of in-person events. Without the need to travel you can book fascinating keynote speakers, create panels of experts, and host a regular travel series with very little logistics and lead-time.

Chapter 4

The Sales Shift

The sales shift is different from the other three. The other shifts (Mindset, Customer, and Performance) are about having an epiphany that inspires you to make important changes to how you approach your travel business. They happen after some deep reflection and a single moment in time where you stop everything and reexamine your approach, make changes, then press on, full steam ahead.

The **Mindset Shift**, for example, causes you to rethink everything about how you view your business and your life according to your vision, purpose, and service.

The **Customer Shift** is significant because it's the result of connecting your purpose with who you want to serve. It creates a rethink, a restart, and a "stop doing" list. You need to let customers who are draining go, and refill your business from the *bottom of your heart, up.*

The **Performance Shift**, as you'll read about in the final chapter, is an overall transformation. It's a system of setting yourself up for a higher level of performance. It's not difficult but requires discipline and deep work, such as setting time aside to set goals and create priorities.

The **Sales Shift** is far more subtle. It does not require a leap of faith. It's not about improving sales with a high-risk move that could put your business in jeopardy. The Sales Shift is a steady, continuous climb up the "skill staircase". It's like a one way escalator. Once you learn a new skill, you rise to a new level, never to return to not knowing how. You keep climbing while gaining more confidence, more customers, and higher commissions. At the top, you reach the Millionaire's Club, only to discover there's another staircase, and another level still to come! It goes on forever because there is always something more to learn.

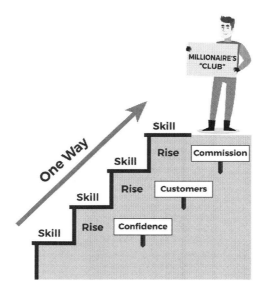

It's easy to assume you're doing okay in the sales department and that you don't have that much to gain. *Or is it?* After all, most of us come into travel with some level of sales skill. When we enter the magnificent world of travel with products that "sell themselves" it's easy to see why sales training takes a backseat to other, shinier offerings such as social media or supplier product training.

Yet I firmly believe that by investing in your sales skills, you'll not only see an immediate return on your effort, but you'll make significant and life-changing gains. Over time, slight and continuous improvements in sales skills will **permanently** place you in a different stratosphere of sales performance.

There are countless examples of when the slightest improvements in your sales skills can make a dramatic impact on revenue. Up-selling to suites, suggesting add-on tours, asking about additional traveling companions, or requesting a referral are a few examples. In fact, choose any step in your sale process, and commit to improving it or doing one more action consistently well, and there will be an immediate, lasting, and scalable benefit. Do it once, and it translates into hundreds of additional dollars in commission. Do it well every time, with every customer, and your sales impact can be in the millions of dollars.

Sales training helps you break through barriers and jump many levels in your sales volume.

Once you heighten your awareness of how you can improve,

and begin implementing changes, you will amaze yourself!

Over the years, I've witnessed hundreds of advisors who've done a complete turnaround in their sales conversions by adding one or two simple, yet effective skills into their process.

I think of Mr. Banks in the movie 'Mary Poppins'. He's a grumpy fellow who doesn't have much time for anyone, even his family. Suddenly, with a "spoonful of sugar" from Mary Poppins, he sees the light! Imagine you find a new and better way to sell. You adjust your sales approach, and suddenly it works! You upgraded clients to a suite, closed your first expedition cruise, or sold a world cruise. It feels like a spoonful of medicine! A thrill rushes over you, and makes you want to take the afternoon off, like Mr. Banks. You broke through a barrier, with flying colours. So, without further ado...

Let's go fly a kite, up in the atmosphere, up where the air is clear, let's all go, fly a kite!

If you want to sell more, earn more, and have more time to travel, the answer lies in your sales skills. If you want more profit, better customers, and a bigger business, improve your sales game.

If you're stuck at a certain sales volume and can't break through, time spent on consistently improving a single sales skill can literally double your revenue.

While the saying, *"Sales solves all problems"* may be an exaggerated truth, it emphasizes the point that more time spent on sharpening your sales skills will always move your business ahead.

Yet in my experience, most travel advisors don't spend enough time improving their sales skills. There is a natural resistance to sales because you don't want to appear too pushy. As a result, it is important to reframe sales training as professional customer service, where good sales techniques *is* good customer service.

Picture an imaginary barrier between you and the multimillion-dollar producer in your office. No matter what you try, you can't seem to ever break through into their club.

When I was growing up, I was a figure skater. I was never going to be an olympic athlete, but my parents kept me in it because they believed in balancing sports with academia. Through skating, I learned the important life skill of practicing something every day where I could see the benefits of making slight improvements.

I progressed through all the basic skills and loved free skating to Elton John early in the morning, but I had hit a wall when it came to landing jumps. For over a year, I had been practicing an axel. In my mind, I couldn't contort my body into the correct position to take off on my left leg going forward, spin one-and-a-half rotations in the air, and land on my left leg backwards. I tried and tried what felt like thousands of times, but became so discouraged that I thought there was something wrong with me.

It didn't help when I watched younger skaters almost get it on the first try. Those who successfully landed an axel were part of an unspoken elite group in figure skating. I was perpetually on the outside looking in.

Seeing my frustration, my parents moved me to a new figure skating coach. Her approach was not to focus on the technical aspects of figure skating. She assured me that I had all the ability in the world to land an axel. She said the problem was that I wasn't making the visual connection to landing the jump *in my mind*.

She had me take the time to visualize the jump. Over and over again, she had me picturing my body taking off on one foot, spinning through the air, and transferring my weight onto the other foot to land the jump. The next step, she said, I was to stick that other foot out to land no matter where I was in the jump. This was a game-changing solution. In my mind, each requirement of the jump had to be done in order. It never dawned on me to stick my landing leg down before I'd finished rotating.

After a full year of jumping hundreds of times and getting nowhere near the landing, I was suddenly landing every jump. They were shaky at first, but my brain finally made the connection on *how* to land the jump. My confidence grew, and I knew I had a new skill that could never be taken away.

I will never forget how it felt to finally land those jumps. My entire body felt the joy of success. I also felt like I'd gained entry into a new club: those who can land an axel. I was finally inside, and I'd never been so proud or happy to be part of a club that I'd earned my way into.

I learned two important lessons. The first was to work with a coach who can help you see a different way of doing things — especially if you know something's wrong, but you can't pinpoint it.

Secondly, once you have a new skill, there's a complete rush of benefits that you had no idea you were missing out on. Maybe you become the agent that suppliers seek advice from or invite to inaugurals. Perhaps you start being singled out for recognition by your host or consortia. Or maybe it's feeling proud of yourself for breaking through the barrier and breathing that rarified air of a top producer. When agents get into a top producer club, they feel like I did when I finally landed that axel: *"It is different up here, and I'm never going back!"*.

The Three Stages of the Sales Cycle

There are three stages to a sales cycle: customer attraction, customer service and customer retention. Let's look further into all three.

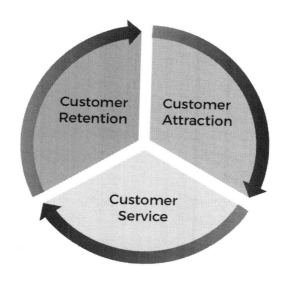

Customer Attraction

The sales cycle begins with **customer attraction.** Customer attraction includes all the steps you take in the sales cycle to engage customers in a vacation conversation. These skills can include prospecting, promoting, reaching out, and asking for an appointment to discuss a client's bucket list. Customer attraction is critical as it is your lifeline to ensuring that you have future sales that you can bank on coming down the pipeline. You will find being proactive, setting time aside in your calendar, and reaching out to at least five prospects per week can make all the difference in the world to your sales.

According to John Assaraf, real estate expert and researcher, top selling agents who earn over $750,00 a year in commission spend 75% of their time in front of clients. When he asked other agents why they were reluctant to spend more time talking to clients, they said that, while they knew it to be less productive, they were more comfortable doing all the other "work".

Does this sound familiar? Even though we all *know* the answer to more sales is more time talking to prospects, reaching out is still an uncomfortable part of the process. Your goal is to do the work to overcome that barrier so that it becomes comfortable for you. Getting in front of prospects is the only way to become a top seller. I promise you, there is a way to reach out and make those calls that is both warm and welcoming.

Customer Service
The second stage of the sales cycle happens after you engage prospects in a vacation conversation and they say "yes!". The first step in customer service is an effective sales process. You lead them by qualifying their needs, making recommendations, and closing the sale.

The next step within customer service is delivering on everything you heard during the sales process. The two steps of effectively leading the sales process and delivering on raised expectations are inextricably linked. That is why sales is such an important part of customer service.

Customer Retention
Finally, after delivering the kind of service that gets clients

talking, the third stage involves customer retention. It includes a follow-up with every client when they return home from their vacation. This includes deep listening for what went well and what they would do differently the next time. Securing a "next call date" to discuss their next vacation is also done during this phase. If you skip this, it makes it harder to reach out in the future.

The best way to assess where you need to improve your sales skills is to understand the ultimate goal of selling. Or, as Stephen Covey says, *"Begin with the end in mind"*. Your "end" is a database full of loyal customers who think of you as *"My* Travel Advisor".

Once you've found your ideal customers, your goal is to treat them as *customers for life* from the very first sale. For example, in real estate, agents spend hours and hours with a first-time homeowner because as they grow their family and income, this client will need a bigger home and will become a repeat customer.

As a travel professional, you need to treat all first-time clients the same way. If you exceed expectations on their first booking by matching the right customer to the right brand, you build a lifelong relationship.

The sales process is exciting because it's where you get to really show your stuff! When you lead a client through the sales process and deliver more than they could ever ask for, you create a raving fan. Not only will they book again, they'll bring their friends to enjoy the same level of service!

Let's review each stage in a bit more detail.

Attracting Clients Through Prospecting

Prospecting is the stage that most of us avoid, especially if it's a cold call. But reaching out to clients is an important part of your service promise. As the advisor, you own the customer journey. Clients depend on you to let them know when the time is right to start discussing their vacation options. Prospecting is part of the entire experience of working with you.

What can make prospecting easier and far more successful is if you set up your clients to **expect to hear from you as part of your service promise**. Booking a "next call date" with every customer sometime in the future helps them expect to hear from you. A next call date gets booked into both calendars so that you never have to make a cold call.

Another way of "warming up" the call is by giving the clients a nudge that you'll be calling. An agent I know sends an email to ten customers every Friday, stating that she'll be calling the following Tuesday to check in on their vacation plans. This not only gives her clients a heads up, it commits her to her weekly phone calls. She says that her clients LOVE hearing from her. In fact, if they can't make it they are quick to give her an alternative date and time.

If you're building your mailing list, reach out to "warm

leads" that you've touched through networking, marketing, and social media. There are a multitude of ways to make friendly connections that make it then much *easier* to call. Ultimately, prospecting is an important part of the successful sales process. Don't skip it!

Active Listening

Remember in school when the teacher said there would be a pop quiz at the end of the lesson? You sat up straighter and paid better attention to the rest of what the teacher was saying.

Similarly, if you listen to customers or even family members with an intent to process what you've heard, you listen much better.

Active listening is when you participate in your client's conversation by taking notes, asking questions, and playing back what you've heard. It's a powerful way of acknowledging what's been said. You'll also discover how you rarely have the important notes exactly right. Even if you restated exactly what was said, the client will often make adjustments when they hear it said back to them. For example:

> **Agent**: What I've heard you say is that you want more time on this vacation to relax and unwind. You want time for reading and playing golf. You found your last vacation a bit too busy. Have I got that right?

> **Client**: Well, it's not that it was too busy. I loved every

minute of it. It's just that I also need time to relax.

Agent: Ah, so was it not quite long enough?

Client: Yes, if we could do ten days instead of seven, I could fit it all in.

Practice tip: Try this exercise at home. You'll be amazed by how people respond to being "heard" (and how, oftentimes, you don't have it exactly right).

Discovery Questions

In every sales conversation, people drop clues as to what's most important to them for their vacation. If you catch these clues, you can do a fantastic job in making the dream recommendations for their holiday. If you miss them, it can be a disaster.

Traditional sales training focuses on a combination of open-ended and closed-ended questions. Open-ended questions are the who, what, where, why, and how questions. Closed-ended questions get you a "yes" or "no" answer.

Skilled sales professionals use a third type of question called discovery questions. These questions specifically target the spoken and unspoken needs of the vacationer. Simply put, these discovery questions get clients talking so that you can "discover" the motivation behind the trip.

Discovery questions vary in their delivery.

Here are a few examples:

 Thought provoking questions.
These questions get the customer thinking deeply about their responses. They are designed to bring out the main purpose of the vacation, what matters and what does not. Most of all, they get the customer talking. They start with expansive words such as "describe" or "explain". For example:

- Explain the main reason for your trip.

- Tell me more about the last trip you had.

- Elaborate on what went well, and what you would want differently next time.

- Describe your perfect vacation day.

- Tell me, what is on your "must have" list?

- Eliminate what I do not have to worry about on this trip for you.

 This or that questions.
These questions allow you to gain clarity by comparing scenarios so that you understand what matters, and in what order of magnitude. It also broadens the perspective on what the vacation can become.

- Is this 10-day cruise or that 30-day cruise the length you prefer?

- Is this over the water bungalow or that garden view room better for you?

- Would you prefer this extension before the cruise or that extension after the cruise?

3 **"What if" questions.**
These questions get the client to consider possibilities they might never have considered. Play with it lightly to see what they are willing to explore.

- What if we did something special such as a river AND an ocean cruise combined?

- What if we started your adventure right from home and you sailed to Europe on the Queen Mary II?

- What if you tried an expedition cruise as a once in a lifetime experience instead of your usual trip to Florida.

- What if next year or two years from now was your year to do a world cruise?

Questions are the key to unlocking the imagination of your customer. If you don't ask, you don't get.

Discovery questions also capture what matters most to the client so that when you present options, they resonate with what has been requested.

One of the best questions you can ask a client is, "Do you mind if I ask you another question?". Getting more time with you is a gift to the client as it helps them figure out what they really feel.

When you can listen with deep empathy — which means listening until you find the emotion behind their point of view — it helps get to the heart of the real purpose of the trip.

Another benefit to discovery questions is that as much as they're about finding out information, they also *stop you from talking*. This is particularly important in the travel industry because it's so easy to get carried away with your own past experiences. There is certainly a time and a place to share, however, when you're trying to get someone to open up, unless you're empathizing with them, save it for later. One of my favourite acronyms I learned from Leanne Lewis at Double Digit Sales, a company that specializes in sales training, is 'W.A.I.T.' which stands for Why Am I Talking!

The key to asking better questions is simply to *ask more of them*. I find it helpful to take a few minutes before every call and to prepare a list of interesting questions. I don't go through every question like a robot. I ebb and flow through them in response to the natural vibe of the conversation.

The goal of the discovery process is to discover their "vacation why". What are their deeper motivations in life? Is it wellness, family, or giving back? Are they feeling pressured, wiped out, or exhilarated? What gaps do they have in their life that a vacation will fill? What season of life are they in? Are they thriving or merely surviving? The client's mindset matters more than anything else when it comes to travel.

All of this helps you recommend the vacation of a lifetime, every time, because you know what the client's underlying needs are during their particular season of life.

The Art of an Effective Sales Presentation

To stand out, you should have a few special tricks up your sleeve. One of the best ways to stand out is to prepare a professional presentation of the options you would like clients to consider. Using professional letterhead, supplier, itinerary and pricing information neatly laid out in a compelling sales presentation is truly a differentiator.

If your consortia or franchise doesn't provide these for you, I highly recommend Canva, an online graphics design company that will make everything you create look professionally designed and produced.

I've seen a wide variety of quotes, from hand-written emails, cut-and-paste supplier quotes, and everything in between. Not only can this appear messy and haphazard, but it can lead to quoting errors.

If you're quoting a $10,000, $20,000 or $100,000 vacation, it's a serious financial investment. The presentation should match the high quality of the vacation.

Here are six tips to make your sales presentations more compelling:

 Avoid providing options in the same conversation as doing the discovery work with the client.
If there is a time sensitive deal that ends today, by all means use that urgency to close the sale. However, if time is on your hands, setting up a future

appointment allows you to prepare a well thought out presentation. The greater the range of options presented, the bigger the value of the sale.

② **Include all decision makers when possible.**
When someone says, "I'll have to run this past my partner", you lose control of what's presented, and you can't get real-time feedback on their objections.

③ **Set the mood for something really special.**
Clients are naturally passionate about taking a vacation. Fuel the anticipation and create a presentation that becomes part of the vacation experience.

④ **Recap their responses to your presentation.**
What stood out for you? What did you hear that was most important? The gift of listening and playing back what you heard them say will help them enjoy the buying experience journey leading up to their decision.

⑤ **Bundle your solution.**
Include as many components of the vacation as you have a solid lead on based on the discovery questions. As we covered in the Customer Shift chapter, bundling differentiates your offer and makes it difficult, if not impossible to compete with. Assume that clients will price shop your offer. Securing the stateroom they want or the last seat on a tour makes

it impossible to match.

6   Include three options.
Have you ever watched *House Hunters* or a real-
estate show? There's a science as to why they offer
the clients three choices; it gives the buyer freedom
and flexibility without overwhelming them.

a)   Offer what they've asked for, even if you don't
believe it's the right choice. If you don't offer them
what they came in asking for, they will feel like they
haven't been heard. Let them come to their own
conclusion as to why it may or may not be the right
fit.

b)   Offer an alternative that has most of what they've
asked for and explain why this second option is a
good fit. Use your notes from their responses to the
discovery questions as close to verbatim as possible
to tie into your rationale.

c)   Offer a luxury option, emphasizing value over price.
Use 'that season of life' perspective to lean into why
this is the right time to indulge, entirely or partially,
in a luxury trip.

Closing the Sale

It seems that after conducting an amazing discovery
process, and making a sensational presentation, closing the
sale would be a done deal. Unfortunately, as shocking as it

might be, it's not.

Often, the reason people don't buy is that your understanding of their commitment is totally different from reality.

People nod and agree, sounding totally committed, but it's possible that you've missed a major clue along the way. Somehow, you've missed the mark. They might be enjoying the discussion immensely, but they aren't convinced.

Or they may be quite committed during the process, but after they leave, something comes up at work. Or family members start weighing in with alternate opinions, and all your work gets derailed. If they leave promising to "think about it", your chances of closing diminish significantly. So does their opportunity to secure the best vacation option you've laid out.

To close the sale, you need to recap the conversation with leading questions towards where you want them to go, and secure an agreement as to where they are in the process.

Questions and Actions

In the closing phase of the sales process, ask specific, closed-ended questions. Like a defense attorney leading the witness in a trial, your closing questions need to lead to the conclusion that the client should buy. Put your hard-earned communication skills to the test. Be bold and clear, and provide direction based on your experience.

Here are examples of closed-ended questions:

- You lit up when we reviewed the condo in Maui and the cruise from Honolulu to Tahiti — that one is available. Why don't I lock it down for you?

- We reviewed three options and most of your questions were focused on the luxury villa. Am I reading you correctly that this is your first choice?

- Based on what you told me about this season of life and your desire to get away, recharge, and explore something new, Option A is the best choice. Are we in agreement that I should book that for you?

- Of all the things we discussed today, what we know for sure is that the Crystal Cruise is the best fit for you. Let's get the cruise booked so we don't lose the suite you love. I'll keep working on your excursions, connecting flights and so on.

Customer Retention

Customer loyalty is a worthy goal. The reason it is so important is that retaining customers is the *payoff* for your hard work and research. After booking clients the first time, you know their travel preferences and which experiences they enjoyed most. You can anticipate the kind of vacation they would likely take next. You can create a series of vacation experiences that build on one another, getting better and better each time.

While customer retention is about keeping the customers that you already have, it is a very active phase in creating customers for life. There may be considerable time between a client's travel adventure from one trip to the next, especially now that the world has been on hold. They may have booked with someone else in between. Retention is not just about retaining them on your email list. It's about refreshing the relationship and attracting them back for a new travel experience. You're courting them anew, even if they've already been with you before.

Repeat customers are also less expensive to attract. According to Forrester Research, a past customer is five times easier to convert into a sale than a new one. You know who your past clients are and where and how to reach them. You don't have to spend money advertising or fishing in a pond of unknown prospects. You can reach out directly at little or no cost.

Finally, retaining customers is the gateway to finding customers just like them. Referrals are the most effective and easy way to multiply your business tenfold.

This *isn't* news to you. Yet, statistics show that as an industry we're getting worse at customer retention, not better. According to suppliers such as Royal Caribbean and Holland America, over 60% of their guests switch agencies between vacations.

Ponder that for a moment. If it's cheaper to retain a

customer, which we know is a pay-off for your hard work and one of the best ways to grow your business exponentially, then why do many agents ignore retention?

They don't ignore it. I've encountered too many hard-working, talented advisors to believe that. However, I do believe that the nature of our industry (with its barrage of endless promotions, a never-ending sea of tasks, and steady demand) makes it easy to lose sight of how important customer retention really is. We are all victims of not realizing how much time has passed since our last contact. Just consider how fast your bi-annual dental check-up comes around!

Here are a few ideas to consider regarding a customer retention strategy that will improve your business:

1   **Know your number and improve it.**
Know what percentage of your clients are repeat clients. This allows you to set a goal and improve on it. Whether you're starting out or pivoting, start with a number that's reasonable, such as 60% or 70%, then aim higher. I know advisors, like our Princess specialist David, who set the goal at 100% repeat or referral clients. Committing 100% sets your thinking and actions in a new direction.

2   **Know your net promoter score.**
Get a clear picture on whether clients will rebook with you by asking them, "Will you book with me

again?" followed by, "Would you recommend me?".
Customer retention experts agree that satisfaction is
best measured by asking those two questions.

Remember to ask this question *right after* you've
completed the booking process. Waiting until after
they travel can be done as well, but the response will
be more about the trip than about the service you
offer. Asking early will also give you an opportunity to
do a customer service 'save' if your client is unhappy.

3   **Be easy.**

Easy to find, easy to book with, easy to do business
with. Customers do business with people who make
their lives easier. Ask yourself these questions:

a)   Am I easy to find? Am I in constant contact? Do
I have an effective website, newsletter, and social
media strategy? Am I the first person they think of
when considering travel?

b)   Am I easy to book with? Do I make the booking
transaction seamless? Do I offer a variety of payment
methods? If the price goes down, do I help clients
with an upgrade or ensure they are getting the best
value at the time of travel?

c)   Do I solve clients' problems? As issues come up, how
do I step in and solve them? Things don't always go
smoothly. At times, a customer wants something that

is no longer available, or they've booked themselves
and find that they made a mistake. Do I stay calm,
stay on top of the situation, and find the best
alternative?

(4) Be creative.
Explore the world on behalf of your clients. Find
new and interesting itineraries, popular trends, and
exciting experiences. Clients are loyal to advisors
who show passion for their work and constantly push
the boundaries of travel.

(5) Apply the golden rule.
Treat every vacation as if it were your own. Consider
each element as if you were taking the trip yourself.
What air would you book? What connections would
you hope for? What experiences are available, and what
similar activities have you done that you can share?

When I interact with travellers at cruise events, I
approach the conversation as if I was traveling with
them. When you use empathy to put yourself in their
shoes, it feels authentic. I know I've hit the mark
when someone asks, "Are you joining us?".

(6) Be appreciative.
Show clients you care by hosting an annual customer
appreciation event. Give awards to your most
traveled guest and for the best travel adventure,
funniest travel story, etc.

"People don't care how much you know until they know how much you care."

~ Theodore Roosevelt

⑦   **Anticipate the next trip before the first one is over.**
Throughout the booking process, consider the trip in the context of the bigger picture of a *lifetime of trips*. Use language that raises the expectation that they will book again and that it *will* be with you. Try these tips:

a)   Prepare them in advance for booking their next trip onboard or during their trip.

b)   Secure a next call date for when they return to review their experience.

c)   Ask them what's on their bucket list and note it in their preferences.

Referrals of a Lifetime

In his book, *The Referral of a Lifetime*, Tim Templeton is emphatic on this point. You don't want or need referrals from every client. You only want referrals when you've earned the right to be referred. Only you can be the judge of that. You'll feel it in your bones when you've exceeded someone's expectations.

In return for that referral, there must be a perceived benefit to the client as well, not the least of which is the benefit of serving as the travel professional who cares as deeply as you do.

Here are five tips on how to create a steady stream of referrals:

1   ***Ask* for the referral when you've earned it.**
If you don't ask, you simply don't get it. Sometimes, it's easy to think that asking for referrals is a hard sell. Yet, if you've invested in outstanding service and people have already expressed their appreciation, it's a natural extension for people to want to "share you" with friends. When you *feel* the gratitude, ask for the referral.

2   **Write out the referral for them.**
Not everyone is born with the writing gene, nor do they have time. When someone gives you praise, acknowledge it by saying, *"Wow, thank you. Do you mind if I write that down as a referral?"* Or summarize what you think they would say and shoot it to them in an email. *"Hello friend, I'm building my online presence and it would be so helpful for me to share your recent experience. I've tried to capture it below — feel free to edit at will!"*

3   **Let them know they're in "The Club".**
Once someone has recommended you or praised you profusely, invite them into your inner circle. Give them a *benefit* of belonging, such as early notification on special travel deals, a customized

newsletter, or an appreciation event.

4. **Some agents create their own advisory boards.**
At a minimum, create a shortlist of your A-listers. Create a cadence of routinely asking for feedback and guidance on key decisions for your business. The ultimate benefit of being a connector is being part of your inner circle.

5. **Reciprocate generously.**
Write testimonials for others. Like and share posts done by your A-listers!

The Sales Shift is an ongoing commitment to doing a little bit better every day. Small changes in how you listen, provide options, and stay in touch keep you in the truly privileged crowd of top-producing travel sales professionals.

The big winners in the end are your clients. Every one of your clients deserves to be guided through an extraordinary sales process that brings their travel dreams to life.

Chapter Summary
The Sales Shift

1. The Sales Shift is a steady, continuous climb up the skill staircase. You never reach the top but with each flight of stairs you land on a new level.

2. Do it once and it translates into hundreds of additional dollars in commission. Do it well every time, with every customer, and your sales impact can be in the millions of dollars.

3. If you want to sell more, earn more, and have more time to travel, the answer lies in your sales skills.

4. Once you have a new skill there's a complete rush of benefits that you had no idea you were missing out on.

5. When agents get into a top producer club they have arrived! "It is different up here, and I'm never going back!"

6. Customer Attraction is critical as it is your lifeline to ensuring that you have future sales that you can bank on coming down the pipeline.

7. Getting in front of prospects is the only way to become a top seller.

8   The two steps of sales and service are inextricably linked which is why sales is such an important part of customer service.

9   Delivering the kind of service that gets clients talking leads to customer retention.

10   Securing a next call date to discuss their vacation is important. If you skip this step it makes it harder to reach out in the future.

11   The "end in mind" is to have a full database of clients who refer to you as "My Travel Advisor".

12   Active listening is when you participate in your client's conversation by taking notes, asking questions, and playing back what you have heard.

13   Discovery questions get clients talking so that you can "discover" the motivation behind the trip.

14   When you can listen with deep empathy — which means listening until you find the emotion behind their point of view — it helps get to the heart of the real purpose of the trip.

15   One of the best ways to stand out is to prepare a professional presentation of the options you would like clients to consider.

16 In the closing phase of the sales process, ask specific, closed ended questions. Like an attorney leading the witness in a courtroom, your questions need to lead to the conclusion that the client should buy.

17 Retention is not just about retaining them on your email list. It's about refreshing the relationship and attracting them back for a new travel experience.

18 You only want referrals when you have earned the right to be referred. Reciprocate generously.

Chapter 5

The Performance Shift — Part One

You now understand that doing what you love for people you love is a critical **Mindset Shift**. You've taken time to consider your ideal customer and how you can dedicate yourself to people who you are uniquely designed to serve, creating the **Customer Shift**. You also know that focusing on your selling skills and doing a little better every day results in a **Sales Shift**. In order to create the greatest impact in your travel business, we're going to pull this all together and create a **Performance Shift**.

A **Performance Shift** is about achieving a seismic result in sales, while at the same time reducing the effort to achieve it. Not only does it increase your commissions, it also reduces your hours of work through continuous improvements. It defines your priorities, hones your skills, and develops strong habits. The **Performance Shift** helps you recognize when enough is enough. You've given it all you've got each day. Renewal is a critical component of this shift, built into it on many levels, so that you never stray too far into overwhelm.

The first step is to get there *before* you get there. What does that even mean?

I am enrolled in a business school called Thought Leaders, out of Australia. They have a ladder of performance that relates to the martial arts.

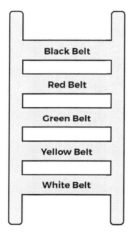

When you first start out, you begin as a White Belt. The further you work through the curriculum and up the sales levels, the further you work up the belts.

The pinnacle is when, at last, you achieve Black Belt. This means that your revenue has reached $1 million per year.

Within Thought Leaders, there is the saying, when someone is establishing a new goal *"What would a Black Belt do?"*, in other words, what would someone who is already selling $1 million in intellectual property do with their day, week, month, or year? Most importantly, *"What would a Black Belt do in this moment?"*.

When I feel tired, frustrated, and like giving up, it helps me to consider a Black Belt's perspective. After all, they are already where I want to be.

A Performance Shift happens *before* you reach the revenue threshold that others have already achieved. It takes into account what other high-performing advisors already do to achieve $1 million, $2 million, $10 million or any level in sales. It builds in priorities, habits, and a path to get you there faster.

What Would a Travel Superstar Do?

In order to get there before you get there, you need to understand how advisors got there before you.

Whatever you're trying to do has been done before. Seek out someone to emulate who is at or beyond the level you're trying to get to. Follow them on social media, and join an association where they (or people like them) belong. If you're attending a conference, join the people who are winning the awards so that their fairy dust rubs off on you.

Here's what I know for sure, after observing thousands of

advisors, including those extraordinary few who break the glass ceiling: there are good and great performers, and then there are *superstar performers*.

Superstar performers have several best practices in common that include having a fabulous attitude, being highly skilled, and being service oriented. The list of ways in which they are amazing is endless.

Superstars hone in on six key strategies which help them stand out:

Superstar Advisor Strategies	Key Actions
HIgh Performance	Organized around priorities.
Constant Growth	Superb sales execution and targeted marketing.
Complete and Profitable Sales Orders	Offer insurance, air, hotel add ons and experiences in a bundled package.
Leverage	A few core suppliers with deep relationships.
Service	Signature customer service that is well documented.

Performance — Organized Around Priorities

Of all the things that set superstar travel advisors apart, organizing around priorities is the one that strikes me as the hardest earned asset they have. Through trial and error, grit, and continuous improvement, a superstar knows what must get done in a day in order to reach their goals.

They have developed rigor and competency around hundreds of tasks. They have an innate understanding of how much is needed to be exemplary, and what is too much or unnecessary.

This discipline of getting things done and knowing how much is enough allows them to save time and improve productivity. The time saved is invested back into improving their business.

Growth — Superb Sales Execution and Targeted Marketing

One of my greatest pleasures is watching a superstar advisor in action with a client. I've seen advisors bring a brochure to life without opening a page. I've heard sales conversations that flow brilliantly like a maestro conducting the string section of an orchestra. I've seen clients light up so brightly, they bring 100 of their closest friends to "come along".

Superb sales execution is the hallmark of a superstar and it is well worth investing in learning how you can improve.

Targeted marketing is an extension of the sales process. The superstar advisor converts sales success into targeted marketing in order to find more customers like the ones who just bought from them. They strike while the iron is hot and leverage their momentum and product knowledge.

Ask yourself, "Who else might love this package?", every time you put something special together. You never know until you ask! One of the great sales endeavors of a superstar is keep asking until you get 100 "no"s.

Complete and Profitable Sales Orders

Superstars climb the revenue ladder by selling more vacation components to each client. They have developed habits around selling upgraded air, excursions, experiences, transfers, tours, and insurance.

While some advisors allow clients to book their air and hotel on their own (because there is less commission), superstar travel advisors book the vacation from "door to door." While the commission on the additional components may be lower, the value of the package increases cumulatively.

Superstars position insurance early on as a best practice for all their clients, offering tremendous peace of mind.

Lastly, superstars put a bow around the package with a service fee that helps their clients feel confident they will work on their behalf.

Leverage — A Few Core Suppliers

Superstar travel advisors invest in fewer suppliers so that they can have meaningful relationships. This allows them to have a deep knowledge of each supplier. It also gives the advisor credibility and a track record when it comes to asking for help. As you know, things don't always go right. A superstar nurtures their supplier relationships so that when things don't go right, they have someone who will take their call.

Superstars make decisions about which suppliers are their "go-to" partners, and they are loyal to that brand. In turn, they can get that upgrade, assistance on a file, and marketing support. They get priority fam trips and even an inaugural invitation or two which in turn reinforces their deep product knowledge.

Signature Customer Service

Customer service is the key differentiator, but superstar travel advisors take it one step further. They push the envelope on creativity and provide special touches from start to finish:

- Presenting documents in a beautiful package

- Making local arrangements for special occasions

- Discounts with local clothing, luggage, or travel accessories

- Connecting with local pet-sitting services

- Reservations at local or onboard restaurants

- Spa services in destination or pre-trip

- Leaving a voicemail on the client's hotel room phone with a restaurant recommendation

- Arranging an essential grocery delivery for when they arrive home and the fridge is bare

- Pizza for the next day when the hard cold truth of no more room service sinks in!

Seth Godin calls these touches "creating your purple cow". They go a long way to helping you be remembered, thought of, and talked about. He says, *"You need a purple cow, something remarkable and exciting, in order to attract attention".*

The difference between a good advisor and a superstar is not trying to do it all. It's about adopting a few key practices, and creating a signature service that you deliver every time.

Chapter Summary
Performance Shift — Part One

1 A Performance Shift is the change that happens when you operate at a higher level, before you get there. It considers what higher performing advisors do to achieve thresholds of $1, $2 or $10 million in sales.

2 Whatever you are trying to do has been done before. Seek someone to emulate who is at or beyond the level you are trying to get to.

3 Superstar Advisors have five key traits that make them stand out.

- **Performance**: Organize and execute around priorities so that they do what is necessary and delegate the rest.
- **Growth**: Consistently grow their business through sales and marketing best practices.
- **Complete the Sale**: Sell the complete vacation experience, including insurance, pre and post options, excursions, air and all other transportation.
- **Leverage**: A few important suppliers that exemplify everything your ideal customer wants in a travel product offering.
- **Service**: Signature service that has your unique "purple cow" experience. It is about adopting a few key practices that you deliver every time.

Chapter 6

The Performance Shift — Part Two

A System for Breaking the Glass Ceiling of Performance

As I was researching this book, I realized that while most advisors have marketing, sales, and technology tools to assist them with their jobs, there is not a great deal of information available on how to improve performance and productivity. Whether you're starting out or hoping to get to a higher level, fine tuning the way you approach your work is as important as the work itself.

This is often referred to as working on your business, rather than in it. It includes everything that impacts the way you do your work including your physical setup, your hours, your energy and time management, the tools you rely on and the company you keep.

I decided to create a resource to assist travel advisors in improving their performance.

The Success Blueprint

The Success Blueprint is a step-by-step process specifically designed to help you achieve your travel business breakthrough. The difference between where you are now and where you want to be are the steps you take to get there, *continuously.*

> *"I'm a firm believer in goal setting. Step by step. I can't see any other way of accomplishing anything".*
>
> ### ~ Michael Jordan

The Success Blueprint has three levels marked by the time frame each takes up in your calendar.

1. Level One — 90 Days

2. Level Two — 30 Days

3. Level Three — 90 minutes

90-30-90 Success Blueprint

Level One:	**90** DAYS	**Vision**	**Priority**	**Renewal**
Level Two:	**30** DAYS	**Target**	**Sprint**	**Reset**
Level Three:	**90** MINUTES	**Focus**	**Commit**	**Rise**
		In View	Interactive	Iterative

The Blueprint is a system to help you grow in ways that light you up over the long haul. It includes small steps over a sustained period of time to achieve remarkable results that matter most to *you*. You could call it a system of **grit**!

According to the best-selling author of 'Grit', Angela Duckworth defines grit as, *"Passion and sustained persistence applied toward long-term achievement, with no particular concern for rewards or recognition along the way. It combines resilience, ambition, and self-control in the pursuit of goals that take months, years, or even decades".*

The Success Blueprint was created to support your travel business breakthrough. It helps you push through the resistance and gives you checks and balances that ensure you reach your goals. You may stall at times, but when you have a system in place, it helps you to keep going, even after you fall.

This system helps you think critically about your choices, and how those choices guide your actions and activities. When your belief system is deeply rooted in a passion for travel, it's easy to overlook important elements, like hours of work and pay. Having a performance system helps you make choices that help increase customer satisfaction *and* increase your financial well-being.

Success depends on much more than a dream. To be successful in the travel business, you need to constantly address the **"too busy"** factor. Too busy checking multiple offers, too busy on hold, too busy chasing refunds. You're always serving clients and rarely serving yourself, not realizing that in serving yourself you would actually be serving your clients better!

Often, you get caught up in the whirlwind of a million things and leave at the end of the day wondering where the time went.

The Success Blueprint takes into account the never-ending tasks included in your day job. It's your system, and your way to get these tasks done by getting them out of your head, and grouped together for the greatest efficiency. It also allows you to manage your energy by doing those things that need to get done during the day like sales or client work when it makes the most sense for you.

The important point is that it *all needs to get dealt with.*
This means doing, delegating, or deleting the stuff that
is taking up space in your head. The Science Foundation
research shows that 80% of our thoughts are negative and
95% are *repetitive.* The Success Blueprint helps you keep
a positive outlook through goal setting, affirmations and
celebrations. It's a tremendous time saver because you think
it once, and act on it accordingly.

The system emphasizes blocking time in your calendar in a
way that makes sense for you. There's a great saying: *don't
show me your priorities… show me your calendar!*

Most importantly, the Success Blueprint helps you take a
stand against time-wasters. Saying "no" to actions that no
longer serve you may be the most important decision of
all. Maybe it's time to say "no" to the tire-kickers and tough
clients, or to using Facebook as entertainment rather than
as a business tool. This is a system that reveals when it's
time to act and when it's time to let go.

Here's how it works:

Timeframe
Most business plans are detailed documents, written when
we're full of enthusiasm and just starting our agency, or as
a refreshing starting point when we're heading into a new
fiscal year. While feeling extremely optimistic and having
the energy to create a masterpiece, as soon as wave season
hits or life gets busy, you rarely give your business plan

another thought!

Goal-planning can also be short-term in nature and given much less attention. I've asked hundreds of agency owners when they do their planning and the answer I hear all too often is, "In the shower", or, "On my way to work". Don't get me wrong; I love a hot water idea! The problem with short-term planning is impatience and the expectation for quick results. You want the idea to both percolate and execute instantly. You want to lose 10 pounds in 30 days, or start a new reading habit immediately that will last. By the end of a long day, instead of pulling out a book, you head over to Netflix with a bowl of ice cream.

Like Goldilocks and her choice of porridge, chairs and beds, the secret to 'planning your planning' is to set your focus and timing intentions right in the middle. Not one year or five years. Not five minutes or two weeks. But in **ninety days**!

The concept of the 90-30-90 planning system is to organize tasks into big ideas and to get them into your calendar. Then to chip away at those ideas via monthly sprints, weekly goals, daily habits, and frequent reviews. Ninety days is far enough in the future to achieve a significant milestone, yet not so far off that you stop counting your steps. Ninety days also fits nicely into the calendar four times every year. It has a built-in, important, and repetitive nature to it.

And hey presto! You can fast-forward four quarters and have an annual plan.

In this chapter we will reveal the secret to pulling all this together in an easy to follow system for high performance.

Impact

After you have considered the timing of your success plan, the next principle to consider is how to create an impact. The Success Blueprint ensures that you account for your time and attention daily, monthly, quarterly and annually.

The more rigor you apply to what does and does not make an impact, the more likely you will be to achieve your goals. There is nothing random about goal achievement. In fact, goal "getting" is a precise practice of balancing the tension between actions, reactions, and continuous improvement.

There are three key questions you should consider when setting your goals. Are they *in view, interactive*, and *iterative*?

In View

You need to clearly see your goals, imagine achieving them, and visualize what your life will be like when your priority is complete. The difference between success and failure can be as simple as writing them down, posting them where you and others can see them, and reviewing them daily.

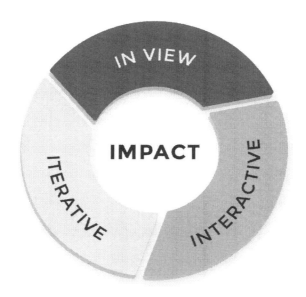

Interactive

Success is not a solo sport. You need to be engaged and to engage others in supporting your dreams. I haven't met a single top producer who did not have an incredible support network. Your planning system needs to be shared and should include key stakeholders and accountability partners who can help you get to the next level.

Iterative

Iterative is a repetitive process where one skill builds upon another. Since both good habits as well as bad habits can build upon themselves, it means taking time on a regular basis to assess the progress you're making before stepping up to the next level.

The Performance Shift: The Success Blueprint Model

The Success Blueprint has three levels, based on its time frame. Level One is 90 Days, Level Two is 30 Days, and Level Three is 90 Minutes. Each level has three stages. Let's break those stages down. As you read through the stages, take time to do the exercises and answer the questions. This will help you put these ideas into practice immediately!

Let's begin!

90-30-90 Success Blueprint

Level One:	90 DAYS	**Vision**	**Priority**	**Renewal**
Level Two:	30 DAYS	**Target**	**Sprint**	**Reset**
Level Three:	90 MINUTES	**Focus**	**Commit**	**Rise**
		In View	Interactive	Iterative

90 DAYS Stage One: Vision

One of the most empowering and insightful things you can do to help you achieve your goals is to create a vision statement. **A vision statement captures what you need to do in the *now* in order to create your future.**

Your vision statement includes an affirmation about where you see yourself in the future, and what steps you must take to get there.

Your *vision* is your view of the future. Your vision-statement on the other hand, is a well-written description of essential steps taken towards *creating* your future. You should be able to write it on a 5 x 7 recipe card , on a white board, or in the front page of your planner. I believe goals are best posted in a printed form of some kind. You may prefer an online version, however it misses the valuable element of having them in plain view. Again, ninety days is a useful timeframe to be long enough to achieve a result, yet short enough that you can easily adapt.

Here are the four key elements needed to create a vision statement for your travel business:

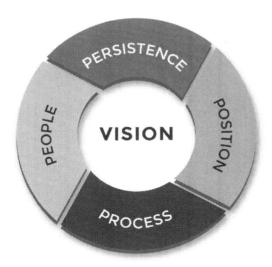

1 Persistence.

The element of doing *whatever it takes* is the difference between being average and being exceptional in the travel business. What three things do you need to do every day, every week, or every month in order to stand out in your market?

2 Position.

Where would you land if you achieved your goals? Your position is like a creative, right brain description of your goals. It is how you describe yourself to the market. Use one of the following statements, filling in the blanks, or create your own.

I am the leading...
I am the best...
I am the exclusive...
I am the top..

3 Process.

Your process is the way you do travel that sets you apart. For example, *"Create memories of a lifetime with every vacation experience"*. Try a few different summary sentences to capture the essence of that thing you do that is truly unique.

4 People.

Who do you serve? Based on your current mindset, goals, passion and purpose, who are your people?

Now that these four elements have been identified, it's time to pull them all together.

Vision Statement

(Persistence) I will _____,

_____, and _____

so that I am: (position) _____

by: (process) _____

for: (who you serve) _____

A vision statement is an affirmation of what you will do in the present state to achieve your desired future state.

Sample Vision One: Luxury Travel Expert

I will invest in luxury training, marketing, and up-selling skills so that I am the most sought-after luxury advisor in my community by curating once in a lifetime, upscale travel experiences for globetrotting empty nesters.

Sample Vision Two: Luxury Villa Travel Expert

I will learn, market and sell, so that I am a renowned luxury villa expert by partnering with Villas of Distinction and other top condo marketers, exclusively for the 60+ market who are concerned with safety.

90 DAYS **Stage Two: Priority**

Priorities are the written catalysts to get you from here to there. They are declarative action statements that say to you and the world, "I'm going to take this action, this way, by this date".

In his book *Prioritize*, Joe Calhoon states that: *"Priorities are the primary tool to accomplish extraordinary results"*. It is a system for organizing your workload around the most important activities. For me, learning how to create priorities out of my endless to-do list was the single biggest change I made in my career in terms of work-life balance.

Priorities are groups of activities that, when done consistently, make the biggest impact in your business. Unlike a to-do list with dozens of tasks, prioritizing groups those tasks together to ensure progress is made. In your work, you can probably set three to five priorities (groups of tasks) every 90 days.

For example, imagine your vision is to be the go-to luxury travel advisor in your community. On a blank sheet you write down all the things that you have to do to make it happen. Stepping back, you start to see patterns such as marketing, training, and servicing.

Each quarter, determine a new priority for each of the big areas that will help you move closer to your vision.

For example:

- Training priority: complete AMA River Academy by January 1st.

- Marketing priority: take a social media course by February 15th.

- Servicing priority: determine my 'purple cow' service and implement with every customer this quarter.

Priorities can also be things you need to eliminate. It's about being intentional regarding your "stop-doing" list.

It's like paddling a canoe. Sometimes, the drag of *not* paddling does more to shift the direction of your boat than rowing twice as hard in a new direction. For example:

- Stop attending webinars for anyone but my core partners.

- Stop multi-tasking on webinars.

- Stop randomly scrolling through social media - only use it to post content and engage with my loyal followers.

Lastly, pay attention to your due dates. If you have multiple priorities, you won't be able to get them all done at once. Stagger your due dates, and be reasonable about the time it takes to get things done. Having a deadline improves your commitment level and helps you measure your progress quarter to quarter.

Selecting priorities is an intentional declaration that you are heading in a new direction, toward higher ground.

Here are a few examples of priorities to inspire you to create your own:

- Complete the Cunard, Seabourn, and Crystal Academies by March 31st.

- Attend the Travel Institute social media training program by June 15th.

- Finalize my sales presentation on my escorted trip to Egypt and present to the local senior center by March 10th.

- Get 100% referrals from each one of my clients by March 1st.

90 DAYS Stage One: Renewal

The journey from here to there can zigzag, slow down, and even stop, as we've seen during the pandemic. Renewal is the process of checking in on your progress to make sure you're on the shortest path to your destination.

When I reflect on the importance of renewal, I think about

swimming across a lake. If you close your eyes and swim as hard as you can, unless you look up from time to time, you can end up going down the lake instead of across it.

The best practice for your travel business is to do a formal review of your progress every quarter.

A renewal is like starting over with a clean slate, but you have the benefit of your past accomplishments to help you move up a level, and build upon what you've accomplished. Reflecting on what you did well and what you would do differently gives you a fresh perspective for setting your priorities for the next 90 days.

Consider checking off your progress like a stoplight. Use green for done, yellow for in progress, and red for incomplete.

Once you have completed your priorities, you can start the process of setting new ones. Some priorities will be ongoing and some will be completely new. Ask yourself the following questions before setting new priorities.

Here is a list of questions to review on your renewal day:

1 **Reflect**
What went well this quarter?

2 What made the biggest difference to my business?

3 What did not go well, and why?

Reset

4 What do I need to do to stay more on track with my purpose?

5 What sprint(s) will I do this quarter?

6 What rewards will I build in when I achieve them?

Renew

7 Where am I on my journey towards my long-term vision?

8 Is my vision statement still on track or do I need to adjust it?

9 Who can I ask for help?

It's helpful if you have a mentor, coach, or accountability partner to do this together with. It's even better when you can sneak away for a day or weekend to somewhere really nice! After all, you are in the travel business!

My husband and I do a renewal each quarter, and support one another in setting and achieving our goals.

Once your assessment is complete, the object of the renewal day is to rewrite your 90-day vision:

> ## Vision Statement
>
> (Persistence) I will _____.
> _____, and _____
> so that I am: (position) _____
> by: (process) _____
> for: (who you serve) _____

Before moving to the next stage, pull out your calendar and select a day for your next renewal. Then complete the vision statement for your next quarter.

90-30-90 Success Blueprint

Level One:	90 DAYS	Vision	Priority	Renewal
Level Two:	30 DAYS	Target	Sprint	Reset
Level Three:	90 MINUTES	Focus	Commit	Rise
		In View	Interactive	Iterative

30 DAYS Stage One: Target

What is a target? Unlike projects and priorities, which are external and require external resources to accomplish, a target is 100% internal. It's within you to achieve or overcome it. It's something you can learn, do, or eliminate in order to get what you want. It's the skills or habits that can take you closer or, if ignored, further away from your goals. A target is made up of skills and habits that you determine as critical to your performance. By definition, according to the Merriam-Webster Dictionary, skills and habits are defined as follows:

- Skill: the ability to use one's knowledge effectively and readily in execution or performance.

- Habit: an acquired behavior pattern regularly followed until it has become almost involuntary.

The target-sprint phase is the gasoline to the vision-priorities race car. Simply put, without working on your skills and habits, you will not win the race.

Ironically, in my entire career, I cannot think of a single point in time where I continuously worked on my skills and habits. I worked hard, completed projects and priorities, but I did not take the time I should have on this phase.

Three years ago, as an entrepreneur, I realized that skill and habit building was essential to my survival. There were so many things I simply did not know how to do. I could not afford to pay someone to do them for me. Now I embrace new skills and habits with vigor, and it has transformed the opportunities I have in front of me. It will for you too!

Let's consider Shelley, a travel advisor who claimed a target head on in order to eliminate a bad habit and develop a new one. An experienced advisor whom I admire greatly, she wanted to get a better grip on her social media habits. This habit grew from checking her online apps and platforms a few times a day, to an almost constant back and forth between each of them.

She considered quitting all together for a long time but lacked the willpower to do much about it. After all, she needed to be on social media for her business as a travel advisor who specialized in wedding groups! How else would she connect with all those excited couples preparing for their big days? Or so she tried to convince herself.

Enter the pandemic, which found her spending hours and hours on social media. The increased screen time combined with the gravity of the situation found her feeling more and more demotivated and discouraged.

At last, it became too much so she decided to quit Facebook and Instagram. However, Shelley quit with a plan in place. She found a fabulous and affordable virtual assistant to do all her posts on social media. Her VA also checked the data, engaged with the comments, and reported back on the progress. Shelley wanted to keep creating the content in order to remain authentic, but at the same time avoid the posting, endless scrolling and checking for "likes".

To her surprise, Shelley instantly felt more productive and engaged both personally and professionally.

By doing this, she repurposed at least two hours per day of unclaimed time. That equates to over a day per week, or almost two months per year! Once she let go of the mismanaged drag of social media in her business, she was able to identify more productive habits.

Targeting is a four-step process. You need to set your sights on a specific skill or habit, do the work to build the skill or break the habit, overcome the resistance and feel the glide.

Let's explore these four stages.

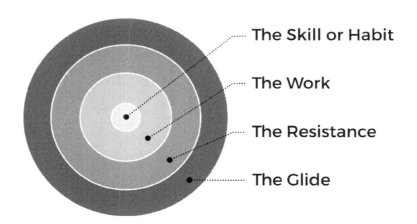

1) The Skill or Habit

First, when selecting a **skill** or **habit**, choose the smallest version of it. Let me share an example. By the time that my daughter was born, I hadn't run for almost two years. The first year was because of the pregnancy. The second year was because of the excuses. I had gained a lot of weight, felt awkward in my body, and didn't think I would be able to finish. The longer I procrastinated, the worse my self-doubt became.

When I finally decided to run, I committed to going to the end of my block. I thought, *if I can just make it out my door, up to the end of the street and back, it's better than nothing.* It was a big struggle. I had no wind, and my legs felt like dead weights, but I ran there and back.

The next day, I was able to run two blocks. A week later, I managed three blocks. In the months that followed, I eventually built up to a 10km run.

For the next two decades, I called myself a *runner*, which gave me so much joy. I found a running partner, built runs into every trip I took, and created a lifelong habit of staying fit and healthy.

I will *never* forget that first bite-size effort to get to the corner of Ruby and Capilano Road in North Vancouver. I can still picture the street sign.

The lasting benefit of a target I made over 20 years ago

is that now, when I take on a new challenge, I think to myself, *"What's the one big goal equivalent to my one block run?"*.

Breaking things down into bite-size pieces works in every area of habit building. For example, if you want to start creating content, try writing every day for 15 minutes. If getting on a healthy diet is a challenge, try removing one treat for one week, then two treats for two weeks, three treats for three, and four treats for the thirty days.

Imagine the smallest version of "just doing it", then go for it! Nobody is watching.

2) The Work

Next, doing the work is just that — *doing the work*. It means showing up at a designated time and working on the skill, or working on improving the habit, no matter what.

It is so easy to get too busy, tired, exhausted, or discouraged. After all, doing the work is a very private exercise. The good news is that nobody knows whether you do the work or not. The bad news is that no one will benefit from your work if you don't do it. You can't serve people if you *don't know how*.

3) The Resistance

Next, you need to **push through the resistance**. There is so much resistance to making progress in your life. There is the external resistance of the day-to-day activities that fill your calendar. There are interruptions, client emergencies, and the real work of your actual day job.

There is also internal resistance, or those stories you tell yourself that you're not good enough or you don't matter. "No one will care if I do this or not." It's a secret battle because often, skilling up and self-improvement feel like they don't matter to anyone else. The truth is, in the short term, they don't mean anything to anyone else but you. Those closest to you will cheer you on, but in the end, it's your game, your rules, and your journey. When it comes to your target, the desire to improve must be stronger than the fear of failure, which can disguise itself as procrastination.

This is why targets are life-changing because you stop putting off what you know deep down is getting in your way.

4) The Glide

The glide happens when what was once hard becomes routine. "I used to struggle selling insurance. Now I bring it up with every client, and can't imagine not selling it... I used to break into a cold sweat when someone asked about a river cruise. I'm escorting one this fall, and another next spring." I have countless stories of advisor after advisor who identified a target, did the work and overcame the resistance to feel the glide.

30 DAYS Stage Two: Sprint

A sprint is a 30-day ritual of continuous self-improvement. Doing something every day without stopping, without exceptions, improves your skill and transforms an idea into a habit.

There is a popular no-carb, no-sugar, no-fun diet called Whole30. My entire family went on it in January 2019. One of its key motivational sayings is, *"It's only 30 days."* Every time I searched something like "Can I eat honey?" or "Can I eat pie?" The Whole30 Guru would return a brief but polite message. *"No, sorry, you can't. But it's only 30 days!".* It was as if there was an unwritten truth that there was pretty much nothing you can't do without for 30 days.

Think of 30 days as a short commuter flight. Soon after the climb of the takeoff, you can feel the descent of the landing. The lure of arriving somewhere you want to go motivates you to keep going, even when you hit some turbulence.

Why 30 days? Why not 21 days, in line with the popular notion of how long it takes to form a habit? According to author and habits expert James Shear, 21 days was a gross misunderstanding and example of an observation being presented as a fact.

Instead, Shear directs us to research done by health psychologist Phillipa Lally at the University College London. On average, it takes more than two months before a new behavior becomes automatic — 66 days to be exact.

We all love short-cuts, and while 21 days seems appealing, the idea behind 30-day sprints is to do them *every* month.

One skill, one habit, one month for the rest of your life. It may seem like a big hill to climb. That's why you need to start small. Like drinking a glass of water every day before lunch.

Your sprint is comprised of the nonstop consecutive actions you take to improve your life. Unlike a goal, where you express the desired result, a sprint focuses on the *effort*. For example, "Lose 10 pounds" is the way most goals are set. A sprint is defined by the daily activity. "Exercise every day". It could be ten minutes or an hour, the sprint gets a tick in the box as long as the exercise is completed.

If you fall off the horse, it's important to get back up and keep riding. In his book *Atomic Habits,* Shear says this: "Never miss twice. If you miss one day, try to get back on track as quickly as possible".

Consider comedian Jerry Seinfeld, who wrote jokes every day for seven years. He didn't care if they were good or bad jokes, or if he was inspired, he wrote every day so that he did not break the chain.

When you break the chain, it's like the boy who took his finger out of the dike. You must plug the hole as quickly as possible and **not miss two days in a row** in order to keep the tidal wave of resistance at bay.

First, decide what you want to accomplish during that 30-day sprint. The key to getting to the next level is to tackle mental blocks that have been holding you back.

"The dread of doing a task uses up more time and energy than doing the task itself."

~ Rita Emmet

People often procrastinate because they don't know how to do one small part of something bigger. Invest in learning how to do the basics of everything in your business. Have mastery over the basics so that the little things don't have mastery over you.

Single targets can be broken down into several sprints, starting with the basics. For example, let's say your target is to become a luxury cruise specialist. For three months in a row, you can use the same target, but work on three compounding skills. For example:

Target: learn product, destinations, deployment, and pricing of luxury lines.

Sprint one (30 days): take all online academies offered by three luxury lines.

Sprint two (30 days): create a compelling sales presentation including a luxury brand with every proposal on Canva.

- **Sprint three (30 days)**: blog or vlog every day for 30 days with tips for luxury travel.

Marie Forleo wrote a book called *Everything is Figureoutable*. Based on observing her five-foot-three mother who could do absolutely anything, Marie developed a philosophy and mantra:

> *"Nothing in life is that complicated. You can do whatever you set your mind to if you just roll up your sleeves, get in there, and do it. Everything is Figureoutable."*

It's true! There is nothing you can't figure out when you put your mind to it. Pick something that's a little (or a lot) beyond your comfort zone that you need to figure out. Then, go for it every day for 30 days *without stopping*.

Stage Three: Reset

The Reset is made up of two elements. First, it's a celebration of your accomplishment of sticking to something for thirty days. After all, It's not easy to stick to a sprint, let alone resist temptation until you feel the glide. A celebration marks what's improved, and what has changed for you beyond the sprint. The act of celebrating is a key ritual on the road to success.

"The more you praise and celebrate your life, the more there is to celebrate."

~ Oprah Winfrey

Secondly, the reset is a chance to go to the next level in your skill staircase by taking stock, and deciding which sprint comes next.

Assess your past sprint and ask yourself the following nine questions:

1. What did I learn in this sprint?

2. What was an unexpected benefit or thing I learned outside the original goal?

3. What did I improve on?

4. What evidence do I have that I've learned this skill or built this habit?

5. What would I do differently?

6. What is the next best skill I need to build on?

7. What habits set me up for success?

8. What distractions made it more difficult for me to finish?

9   Was there a time of day that worked best?

Reset after every sprint with a celebration and an assessment of its impact on you. Identify the greatest lessons learned from applying non-stop action in one direction. I promise, the benefits will far exceed the original expectation of your goal.

90-30-90 Success Blueprint

Level One:	**90** DAYS	**Vision**	**Priority**	**Renewal**
Level Two:	**30** DAYS	**Target**	**Sprint**	**Reset**
Level Three:	**90** MINUTES	**Focus**	**Commit**	**Rise**
		In View	Interactive	Iterative

 ## Stage One: Focus

Focus helps calm your mind, keeps you in the present moment, and sets you up to do your best work. If your vision is your eye to the future, and the target is the internal work horse to get you there, **then focus is your approach to getting things done.**

Focus is how you approach each day to give yourself the best chance of success. Focus is so important that you are going to dedicate 100% of your undivided and uninterrupted attention to it for **90 minutes.**

Most experts agree that this is a morning ritual. Check out *The Miracle Morning* by Hal Elrod, *The 5am Club* by Robin Sharma, and Tony Robbins' priming routine. Each author explains why spending the early hours of the day becoming the best you can be, is the best thing you can do for yourself in order to be in service to others.

Following are three quotes that I keep "in view" to help me focus. The fact is, I have these memorized because I've referred to them so often when coaching myself and others:

> *"Things which matter most must never be at the mercy of things which matter least."*
>
> ~ *Goethe*

What stands out for me is that there needs to be an element of awareness of what matters and what doesn't, what is above the line and below it. By process of elimination, some things rise to the top and others fall away.

"Putting first things first means organizing and executing around your most important priorities. It is living and being driven by the principles you value most, not by the agendas and forces surrounding you."

~ Stephen Covey

Covey also adds the idea of standing firm in your values and protecting yourself from other people's agendas. When you put what matters most in plain view, it gives you a benchmark for measuring everything that is asked of you. It becomes easier to draw the line and say no when what is being asked of you does not support your priorities.

"What's the one thing you can do such that by doing it, everything else will be easier or unnecessary?"

~ Gary Keller

Taking it one step further, and probably the best lens of all for making decisions about what to do next is from the book, *The One Thing*. Gary Keller asks, what is the ONE thing that I can do today that will make the biggest difference AND may eliminate other tasks altogether? We can only do one thing at a time. Often, when the day explodes, there is only time to do one thing. Ask yourself, if I could ONLY get one thing done today, what would it be?

I love the progression of these three quotes. All the great work around priorities is based on the founding work by Goethe and reinforced by the other two. The message is clear. Decide on your most important work. Do not let the unimportant work get in your way.

The 90-minute focus includes two components. The first is the schedule and the second is the work.

The schedule pertains to how you will set up your "perfect day". Jim Loehr and Tony Swartz, author of *The Power of Full Engagement*, stress:

> *"Energy, not time, is the fundamental currency of high performance."*

We are not built to be like computers, processing at high speeds, continuously without breaks.

Go for no more than 90 minutes before taking a break to renew your energy. Take a walk, get some fresh air, and most importantly, step away from the work, physically *and* mentally.

When you block your schedule for the day, consider your energy and the required tasks at hand. For example, do your creative work early in the day if you're a morning person, or at the end of the day if the afternoons help you relax and get into the zone.

The next part of your 90-minute focus is to decide on what matters most *today*, in this moment of your business and life. It makes sense to put your sprint into the first 90 minutes of the day, but it may not always be the single most important thing to get done. Productivity is a constant balance between what needs to get done against the budget of time, energy, and inclination.

During your 90-minute focus, spend your time applying divergent-convergent-divergent thinking. In other words, go broad and consider all the possibilities, then narrow your focus by process of elimination to work on one thing at a time. Then go broad again with creative solutions towards completing your task.

When you try to do things too quickly, you either work on the wrong things or skip the creative genius of considering all the ways to get things done.

Chris Bailey explains this phenomenon in his very useful book, *Hyperfocus*. He points out that there are two cognitive functions that we need to apply: hyperfocus and scatterfocus.

The most recent neuroscientific research reveals that our brain has two powerful modes that can be unlocked when we use our attention effectively: a focused mode (hyperfocus), which is the foundation of being highly productive, and a creative mode (scatterfocus), which enables us to connect ideas in novel ways.

The idea is to apply hyperfocus, getting very clear on the task at hand, *and* scatterfocus, which applies creativity to solving the task.

My perfect day blueprint (credit to Robin Sharma's book, *The 5am Club* for the idea) starts by being scatterfocused, with me writing down my entire to-do list. It allows me to get everything out of my head and down on paper.

Then, I move to hyperfocus — I eliminate, delegate and delete. After years of doing this, I'm getting better and better at knowing what I can get done in a day. It still feels good to get it out of my head and written down as five key tasks.

Every single morning, once I have my five things identified, I write them down on a whiteboard. I have the advantage of working from home. If you're in an office, find a way to write down your perfect day actions (try to keep it to no more than five) and put them in plain view every single day. It's a game changer, I promise.

I start with the ONE thing I am focusing on improving, which is usually my sprint. I spend 60 minutes pushing myself as far as I can go on that one thing. I take time to be creative. I remain open to learning and drifting into new territory if my mood takes me there. I do this at 5am so that there's no rush to starting the other parts of my day. Sometimes I take 30 minutes, and some days two hours go by and I'll still be at it.

Next, I move through the list, sometimes tackling the tough ones, and other times going for a nice easy one.

I also pay attention to my energy. For example, I do creative work in the morning when my brain is fresh, I do sales calls before 10am or they will NEVER happen because, like most of you, I don't find it easy to make sales calls. Then I schedule client work in the afternoon as my "people time" which always boosts my energy.

The 'hand of meaning' is a simple tool for making decisions about what to work on.

Put your dominant hand down on a piece of paper, and trace it using your other hand. The trick is to engage your brain by challenging it to do something it's not used to.

Choose your tasks for the day by assigning them a meaning.

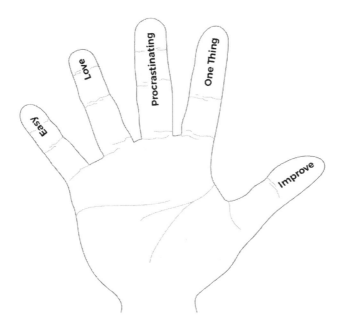

1. Pinky — What's easy?

2. Ring finger — What do I love to do?

3. Middle finger — How am I procrastinating?

4. Index finger — What's the one thing that will make everything else easier or redundant?

5. Thumb — What do I need to get better at?

The key is that this is your perfect day. You'll begin to design your days around what works best for you. It all needs to get done, delegated or deleted. The *next* day ,I reflect back with gratitude on what I accomplished. Some people do this at the end of the day but I am usually too wiped out. My morning ritual always includes a review of my progress, a little celebration, and a fresh new list of what would be my next blueprint of a perfect day.

Create and schedule your perfect day into your calendar. You will have your own template based on priorities, energy levels and sprints. Have fun playing with it to find the right balance for yourself.

In summary, the purpose of the 90-minute focus stage is to master your approach. It becomes a game to set the stage for your perfect day by setting aside the right time, working on the right things, and taking the appropriate breaks, all improving your performance.

90 MINUTES Stage Two: Commit

To commit is to connect actions to your beliefs. It's a message to your belief system that leads you from "I can do this" to *"I AM this".*

Commitment is not a passing thought about doing something, or lip service to getting something done. **Commitment is the action of creating a real *belief*.** It forces you to say out loud and write down, *"I am already there".*

When writing affirmations, consider shifting your language

from the things you want to change (which can feel heavy or onerous) to a confirmation that you *are* changed, which sends a signal to your brain that you're already there.

Look at the following three affirmations and how they have been rewritten:

1. "Be a luxury cruise specialist" becomes, "I **am** a luxury cruise specialist".

2. "Improve my social media presence" becomes, "I **am** a high-profile expert in luxury travel".

3. "Learn how to create better presentations to close more sales" becomes, "I **create** compelling sales presentations" or, "I **am** a closer".

For years, I resisted affirmation statements. The high achieving "doer" in me pushed against the idea of *"think it and it will come"*.

But when I adopted these statements, they became a personal confidence builder for me. In writing 'I am' statements, I observed how naturally I went about making them come true. The science behind affirmations, combined with my own experience, won me over.

According to research lead by Dr. Christopher Cascio and Associate Professor Emily Falk, affirmations access two functional areas of the brain responsible for stimulating the reward response: the ventral striatum and the prefrontal cortex. These are the same reward centers that respond to other favorable experiences such as enjoying a piece of pie or winning a prize. In other words, when you say "I am", your brain believes you.

"*Affirmations* take advantage of our reward circuits, which can be quite powerful", says Cascio. They are also proven to be more powerful than thinking about past successes. In part, this is because we can write a new story, rather than get caught up in the things that did not go well in the past.

This lesson is not new and has stood the test of time.

> *"I doubt therefore I think. I think therefore I am."*
> **~ Rene Descartes (1596 — 1650)**

Once you begin writing "I am" statements, you begin to access your reward center. You experience, at a subconscious level, the satisfaction of the prize. When you write your "I am" statement in the morning, your brain starts scanning your day for evidence that proves that the statement is true.

Start writing things down that feel comfortable, then stretch them out to be aspirational:

- "I am a travel advisor. I am a trusted travel advisor."

- "I am a specialist. I am an expert."

- "I am successful. I am wildly successful."

- "I am a travel expert. I am a travel superstar."

It's also important to offset resistance with affirmations of encouragement.

Try adding these kinds of statements:

- "I am patient", when you're feeling frustrated that you're not getting results.

- "I am thorough", when client work takes all the attention and you run out of time to do everything in your list.

- "I am running my own race", when the comparison monster sneaks in and you're jealous of someone else's success.

- "I am a professional, not an amateur", when your confidence needs a boost.

90 MINUTES Stage Three: Rise

You are born with a purpose, and your purpose is to serve others with your unique gifts. You rise when you are brave enough to answer the call. You rise when you recognize in yourself the courage it takes to not only have a dream, but to openly declare it on a daily basis.

There can be difficult periods where, despite all your efforts, you feel like you're losing ground. Long before the pandemic, there were commission cuts, economic hardships, 9/11, SARS, and so much more. Itineraries change, clients cancel, and worse yet, clients leave us. The cycle of challenges can be exhausting. This past year has been excruciating. My heart breaks for our entire industry. All the more reason we need to keep going, and celebrate the effort and the rewards that will follow.

Rising every day is not easy, but it is important. Rising is doing one thing every day that scares you, and then celebrating it.

One of my mentors, long-time industry legend and Hall of Fame inductee, Michael Drever taught me the importance of rising and ringing the bell every day. When he was an agency owner, he had a Holland America bell installed in the office. He encouraged his team members to ring it every single time they got a booking. He recognized that it is never easy to make a sale and it should never be taken for granted.

It was a wonderful feeling of accomplishment for each advisor who rang the bell, and the entire team would break out in a round of applause. As an added bonus, Michael would know if he was ahead or behind pace on his revenue goals by counting the times the bell rang in a day. A brilliant and simple strategy.

If you've come to the end of your day and haven't rung the bell, take a minute. There is always something to *celebrate*!

You need to rise, be gentle with yourself, and be grateful for the journey. Even the tough stuff is a gift to help you be better tomorrow. Eventually you will rise so high you will pinch yourself. Honor the effort and the results will come.

So, let's raise a glass, check a box, or ring that bell, and do the happy dance at least once a day, *together*. I am with you in spirit! I see you! I hear your bell ringing loud and clear!

> *"The rising tide lifts all the boats."*
> ~ ***John F. Kennedy***

The 90-30-90 Success Blueprint is your armor to fight against average, backslides, and short-lived success. It will help you answer the call, and breakthrough in your travel business.

Chapter Summary
Performance Shift — Part Two

1. The difference between where you are now and where you want to be are the steps you take to get there, continuously.

2. The Success Blueprint helps you push through the resistance and gives you checks and balances that ensure you reach your goals.

3. When your belief system is deeply rooted in a passion for travel, it is easy to overlook important elements, like hours of work and the pay.

4. To be successful in the travel business, you need to constantly address the "too busy" factor.

5. The important point is that it all needs to get dealt with. This means doing, deleting or delegating the stuff that is taking up space in your head.

6. Saying "no" to actions that no longer serve you may be the most important decision of all.

7. The concept of the 90-30-90 planning system is to organize tasks into big ideas and to get them into your calendar.

8. There are three key questions you should consider when setting your goals. Are they in view, interactive, and iterative?

a. You need to clearly see your goals, imagine achieving them, and visualize what your life will be like when your priority is complete.
b. Success is not a solo sport.
c. Iterative is a repetitive process where one skill builds upon another.

9. A vision statement is an affirmation of what you will do in the present state to achieve your desired future state.

10. Priorities are the primary tool to achieve extraordinary results.

11. Renewal is the process of checking in on your progress to make sure you are on the shortest path to your destination or goal.

12. A target increases your ability to get closer to your goal by improving in a specific area. Unlike priorities or projects which tend to be external, a target is internal.

13. Targeting is a four-step process. You need to set your sights on a specific skill or habit, do the work to build the skill or break the habit, overcome the resistance, and feel the glide.

(14) A sprint is a month-long ritual of continuous improvement. Doing something everyday without stopping, without exception, improves your skills and turns an idea for improvement into a habit.

(15) The reset is made up of two elements. It's a celebration of what you've accomplished and then, by taking stock, a decision on what your next sprint will be.

(16) Focus is the antidote to overwhelm. If your vision is your eye to the future, and the target is the internal work horse to get you there, then focus is our approach to getting things done.

(17) "Energy, not time, is the fundamental currency of high performance." Jim Loehr and Tony Swartz.

(18) Our brain has two powerful modes that can be unlocked when we use our attention effectively: a focused mode (Hyperfocus), which is the foundation of being highly productive, and a creative mode (Scattterfocus), which enables us to connect ideas in novel ways. Chris Bailey

(19) To commit is to connect actions to your beliefs. It's a message to your belief system that leads you from "I can do this" to "I AM this."

(20) You are born with a purpose, and your purpose is to serve others with your unique gifts. You rise when

you recognize in yourself, the courage it takes to not only have a dream, but to openly declare it – daily.

Conclusion

The goal of becoming *my* travel advisor for people you care about and serving them with everything you've got, is a noble ambition. It's worth answering the call to face your fears and make changes that lead to a lasting impact.

The pandemic, with all its devastation and uncertainty, has forced a new future of travel upon us. You have an unprecedented opportunity to create your version of it, like never before. Some travel advisors are going to get into the same car, with all its dents, scratches and the engine light on. You on the other hand, have traded yours in for something brand new. It's faster, bolder, and more magnificent than before. Your new travel business is built for high performance!

The first gear is a **Mindset Shift**. The vision you have for your future is unlimited! It's a motion picture of yourself doing what you love, with people you love, earning what you're worth! It's both fun and profitable. Your new travel business is built on purpose. You're going to do the travel business your way. Your unique ability sets you apart from the rest. Your purpose is the ultimate competitive advantage because only you can do you! Your purpose will draw the people you are designed to serve. Your service promise is your signature trademark that people value and are willing to pay for.

The second gear is the **Customer Shift.** It's about working from the *bottom of your heart, up.* At the heart of your business, there is a single avatar that exemplifies everything you want in a customer. Finding your customer avatar is a key breakthrough because it creates a singular focus for your travel business.

It provides leverage for your training, marketing and service. Learn it once, sell it often, and suddenly there is far less work for the money.

The next gear is the **Sales Shift**. It is a tremendously important part of the customer experience. A customer that has been sold well is far better off because they have been given your undivided attention. The **Sales Shift** pertains to continuously improving, even by the slightest degree, every step in your sales process. Making one small change for the better can mean hundreds of dollars in revenue on a booking. Make that change on every booking and it can mean millions of dollars to your business.

The last gear, which will put you on the superstar advisor proven path to success, is the **Performance Shift**. You can 10x your business, without working harder. The secret to high performance is in your approach to the business. Once you've made the key shifts in Mindset, Customer, and

Sales, the last and critical step is that you put these into a framework that moves you from a goal setter to a goal getter.

The Success Blueprint is a step-by-step approach to BIG goal attainment.

The new insights shared in this book will help you realize that you don't have to be *all things to all people*. If you boil your travel business down to one important client, if you serve them by giving them your undivided attention, before long, as Walt Disney said, they will bring their friends to see you do it!

The final thought to ponder is an important one. Becoming *my* travel advisor is not something you can ask for or assume. It must be *earned* and re-earned. It is an esteemed badge of honor that brings uncommon loyalty. Put yourself in the shoes of your ideal customer and imagine how they feel when suddenly they are the subject of your pursuit in becoming *my* travel advisor. They feel like they matter, which is all anyone really wants. That's what makes doing travel business this way such a worthy endeavor.

You've got this! I believe in *you*.

About the Author

As an experienced SVP, I led Sales and Supplier Performance for the Expedia Cruises organization for over a decade. I was also a senior leader with Princess Cruises and Travel Market Report.

Three years ago, I made the leap into entrepreneurship and started my coaching practice. Although I've been coaching my entire career, I decided that helping people achieve their dreams is my life's work.

I work with organizations, leaders and travel advisors who want more from their business and their life. If you're stuck, overwhelmed, or can't seem to get what you've always wanted, work with me!

What stands out about me is that I have led from every seat at the table, from frontline sales to executive leadership, owner, and solopreneur.

I'm the person you reach out to when you don't know who to ask!

Connect with Me

It is my sincere hope that this book has inspired you to make the changes you need to create the travel business you've always wanted.

Whether you're a travel advisor, agency owner or industry professional, I'm passionate about helping you make an impact!

I believe that together, we can change the industry, and help make the world a better place, through travel.

Here are a few ways to connect with me.

 Newsletters
The Shift Room — An exclusive newsletter for travel advisors

On Leadership — A newsletter to help courageous leaders rise up

Sign up at **www.geraldineree.com**

Follow me as I provide relevant, timely insights to help you on your journey.

(2) Coaching
If you're looking for professional coaching, I have a variety of programs to choose from including one-on-one, group coaching, and achieving peak performance as a team.

(3) Strategic Planning and Facilitation
I help organizations shift into a new direction, lead change, and achieve BIG goals through strategic planning and team building workshops.

(4) Event Speakership
One team, one voice, one vision. A compelling agenda with riveting and relevant content is the difference between a good event and an event that your audience will talk about for years to come.

I help organizations transform events from the best of the year, to the best ever!

www.geraldineree.com

Manufactured by Amazon.ca
Bolton, ON

25907518R00118